Health Analytics

Wiley & SAS Business Series

The Wiley & SAS Business Series presents books that help senior-level managers with their critical management decisions.

Titles in the Wiley & SAS Business Series include:

For more information on any of the above titles, please visit www.wiley.com.

Health Analytics

Gaining the Insights to
Transform Health Care

Jason Burke

WILEY

Library of Congress Cataloging-in-Publication Data:

Burke, Jason, 1969-
  Health analytics : gaining the insights to transform health care / Jason Burke.
      pages cm. — (Wiley and SAS business series ; 60)
  Includes index.
  ISBN 978-1-118-38304-9 (hardback) — ISBN 978-1-118-73427-8 (ePDF) — ISBN 978-1-118-73395-0 (ePub)
  1. Health services administration—Decision making—Mathematical models.
2. Health facilities—Business management.   3. Medical care–Information technology—Management.   4. Medical informatics—Management.   I.   Title.
  RA971.B87 2013
  362.1068–dc23

2013015634

Printed in the United States of America

10 9 8 7 6 5 4 3 2 1

Contents

Foreword

Medieval cartographers, whenever they attempted to map areas of the globe that they didn't understand well, marked "Here be dragons" or "Here are lions" on entire continents. Their intent was to suggest to travelers that they weren't sure just what perils might be encountered in these unexplored regions. Anyone venturing to Asia or Africa was thereby warned to look out for dangerous beasts of various types.

When we travel in the world of contemporary health care today, there are unexplored dangers at every turn. We spend far more money than our outcomes justify. We get lost among the fragmented silos of providers, payers, and life sciences manufacturers. New science and care protocols emerge daily, leading to more complexity than most practitioners can comprehend. Every dramatic new development, from personalized genetic medicine to robotics and telemedicine, opens up new frontiers, but confuses patients and their caregivers.

One of the most powerful new developments in health care is the use of analytics to help make decisions. This new tool has the potential to shed considerable light on the entire terrain of health care. When executed well, analytics can tell us who is likely to acquire particular diseases, which treatments work for which patients, and how much a treatment protocol should—and does—cost. Data and statistics can shed light on which provider organizations—and even which individual providers—are doing a good job. They can even begin to bridge the large gaps between industry sub-segments, providing a much more comprehensive perspective on patient care processes, spending, and outcomes. In short, health care is poised on the edge of an analytics-driven transformation. Should we jump? After you've read this book, your answer will be "Yes."

We will need guides and maps for this transformative journey, and Jason Burke is our experienced cartographer for this relatively unexplored territory. He's well suited to play this role, having founded and led a research center for health analytics at SAS, which is the leading provider of analytics software. I worked with Jason at the International Institute for Analytics, where he was one of the faculty members, and I found his thinking and writing to be consistently clear and thoughtful.

I use the cartographic analogy for a reason. At the center of this book is a map of the health analytics territory—a taxonomy of the things a health care organization can do with analytics. When I saw the first version of this map a few years ago in one of Jason's blog posts, I was immediately struck by its usefulness. I remember thinking to myself at the time that the taxonomy would provide a great structure for a book. While it's not by any means the only framework Burke employs in the book, it does underpin several of the early chapters.

There are many different questions that the map can help to address. When I work with companies—regardless of industry—on analytics, one of the key issues is always where to start and how to evolve. As Burke makes clear, there are many different areas of health care to which one can apply analytics. Do you want to improve clinical practice? Understand and improve financial results? Provide greater operational efficiencies? You might want to do all of these things with analytics, but you can't do them all at once. The map lays out all the options for health care organizations to decide among. Just like tourists traveling in Europe, who need to prioritize what cities and countries to visit, health care executives need to prioritize their analytical initiatives, and Burke's map will be an invaluable guide.

Burke realizes that analytics can be a scary subject for many readers, so he has avoided jargon and technical terms. I'm a big fan, not only of the map, but also the four capabilities he lists that health care organizations need if they're going to be successful with analytics. One of the four—high-performance computing—ventures into the fashionable but poorly understood world of big data. Burke treats this topic like all the rest—in a calm, sober fashion. He knows that big data in health care will simply be added onto a variety of other technologies and issues, and that there is no value in treating it as a separate subject.

Like it or not, health analytics is a long-term journey for any organization wishing to undertake it. But like other long trips, it will be accomplished through a series of smaller steps. By breaking down and illuminating the territory of health analytics, Jason Burke makes it possible for any organization to understand the options, make a plan, and demonstrate progress. Analytics will bring a revolution to health care, but there will be many evolutionary advances to get us there.

THOMAS DAVENPORT
Distinguished Professor, Babson College
July, 2013

Preface

When it comes to writing a book about health care, it is a lot harder these days to decide on the topic. Do you talk about the crippling impact of ever-rising health care costs? Or perhaps the implications of U.S. health reform legislation on national and international health care markets and business models? Another approach might be to focus on the need for performance-based incentive structures in driving health delivery transformation. Or how medical tourism and the rise of the informed health consumer are driving changes in behaviors for both businesses and consumers. You could even spend a few pages talking about the effect of doubling the health IT market size through federal subsidies and incentives. The list of potential topics is pretty long, and the picture is evolving at an unprecedented rate. The only absolute certainly is this: the future practice of medicine will look considerably different than the model prevalent in the 20th century.

This book is about painting a tangible picture of a different future for health care—one where the business of health care is more closely connected to the evolving science of medicine and the evolving role of individual health care consumers (i.e., patients). It builds the case for a fairly singular idea; namely, that using health-related information in new and creative ways can dramatically lower costs, enhance profitability, improve patient outcomes, grow customer intimacy, and drive medical innovation. We call this opportunity "health analytics."

Why do we believe health analytics offers such an opportunity? Well, for starters, other industries take advantage of advanced analytics every day. These industries have already made major shifts in becoming information-based businesses. Though the journey is never over, the world of proven possibilities is extensive. And we believe it is the responsibility of every health leader today to identify and learn from those experiences in other markets.

Another reason we believe in the opportunity for health analytics is that consensus is emerging within the health and life sciences markets about what a modernized health enterprise will look like—and it looks highly information driven: collaborative, cost-aware, and outcomes-oriented.

Collaborative. Whereas the historical view of health communication involved one-on-one exchanges between two or three practitioners, health care delivery will become truly collaborative. Multiple practitioners across institutions will work together to develop and monitor treatment programs for their patients. Providers, researchers and payers will learn how to maximize health outcomes at the individual patient level. And patients themselves will be active collaborators and contributors to their own therapies and wellness efforts.

Cost-aware. Without question, the single largest driver of health transformation is cost. In a climate dominated by unsustainable expenditures and expensive inefficiencies, no one has benefited: patients unable to pay skyrocketing premiums and prices, payers unable to financially manage risk, and providers unable to profitably maintain the practice of medicine. All constituents in the modernized health system must become more fully cost-conscious in terms of efficiencies, incentives, discretionary spending, risk management and quality.

Outcomes-oriented. The top care providers have always sought the best health outcomes for their patients. But a modern view of health outcomes is multidimensional. Efficacy, sustainability, prevention, quality, safety, and cost all represent important facets of health outcomes. So while the betterment of patient lives is always a primary concern, a more comprehensive view of health outcomes will be required to support the care delivery model.

In short, creating a collaborative, cost-aware, outcomes-oriented health care system requires embracing an ability and priority of information-based decisions.

EMBRACING HEALTH ANALYTICS

The term we use to describe this opportunity for transformation is "health analytics." But we use this term with some trepidation.

By any objective measure, the term "analytics" is loaded. It is an over-used term that has been associated with an unbelievably broad set of concepts. In the minds of many executives, analytics can mean one of two less-than-comfortable things: either a set of simple reports that have yet to be a useful catalyst for fundamental change, and/or a mathematical discipline requiring highly specialized people that are certainly in small numbers if found on their employee rosters at all.

This book seeks to disentangle the concept of analytics—especially advanced analytics—in the context of health care. We will not be discussing complex mathematical models, sharing any software code, showing you a better way to construct a Web report, or describing a set of unattainable business capabilities. This book is not about setting the stage for big consulting projects or explaining why the massive technology infrastructure you already have is insufficient.

Our goals are simple. First, we want to more fully define, in terms relevant to nontechnical business leaders, a new health care ecosystem powered by information. Second, we want to establish the core capabilities that enterprises will need in order to operate successfully in that new health ecosystem. Third, we want to provide sufficient examples of these concepts actually being applied to prove that what we are describing is actually attainable and not science fiction. And lastly, we want to outline a road map—one that any enterprise can follow to assess their current ability to participate in this new health ecosystem, and plan how to grow those capabilities over time.

A FUTURE IN INSIGHTS

The applications of analytics to improving health outcomes and costs are limited only by the imaginations and motivations of the people enabling change. And the opportunity for innovation is astounding. More importantly, though, the journey to fully utilizing health analytics to drive health transformation is just beginning. In addition to dealing with the practical aspects—data integration, quality management, computing capacity, governance—institutions must also face up to the changes in organizational capability and culture that accompany any evolution of this type. It is a tall order, but through the ideas captured here, you will see that this is not some far-off future. Organizations are successfully making the transitions today and reaping the benefits of a more fully empowered, efficient, and even profitable health enterprise.

Acknowledgements

I t is impossible to list all of the people who have helped, encouraged, and supported me in my quest to raise the quality of questions we are asking of our health data. But there are a few I wanted to make sure I mentioned.

In 2011, SAS launched an initiative called the Center for Health Analytics and Insights (CHAI). The goal of this ambitious effort was to assemble a group of industry professionals to research and prove how existing advanced analytical capabilities could be applied to solve health and life sciences problems in new and creative ways. The initiative was supported by a wide variety of executives at SAS, including Dr. Jim Goodnight, Carl Farrell, Kecia Serwin, Dan Cain, and Michael Hower among many others. Without their support, I would not have had the opportunity to build, lead, and collaborate with many of the talented people I acknowledge in the following paragraphs.

As part of building CHAI, I was fortunate enough to meet and hire Dr. Graham Hughes as our Chief Medical Officer. Beyond his obvious contribution to this book (he wrote Chapter 5), Graham has been a wonderful friend and colleague who has consistently supported and shared my beliefs in the opportunity for analytical innovation. I'm grateful for his spirit, intellect, collaboration, and friendship.

Innovation projects notwithstanding, the best part of CHAI is the people. My colleagues in CHAI have included (in alphabetical order) Bassel Abu-Hajj, Cindy Berry, Walter Boyle, Carol Dorn Sanders, David Handelsman, Gary Kohan, Dr. Jiacong Luo, Dipti Patel-Misra, Sarah Rittman, Chris Scheib, Brad Sitler, Alice Swearingen, and Anne Wiles. I am grateful for their creativity, energy, and commitment to moving our industry toward more data-based decision making.

I'm also very grateful to Tom Davenport for his pioneering work in raising the awareness of how analytics can and should be driving better business results across all industries, including health care. His books on analytics should be required reading for every 21st century health executive, and his work with the International Institute for Analytics has provided one of the few forums for the exchange of business experiences and ideas related to analytics. And I'm especially grateful for his contribution of the Foreword to this book.

The publishing teams at Wiley and SAS provided great support to me on this project. I am especially grateful to Stacey Hamilton for her oversight and management of this project, and for Shelley Sessoms for getting the ball rolling.

This book has been a labor of love for me, but it took my time and attention frequently away from home. I am sincerely grateful to my wife Christina and daughter Hadley for their love, support, and many sacrifices that gave me the opportunity to do this work.

Throughout this book, I've incorporated specific industry examples that illustrate some of the topics being discussed. People who have never had the experience of working in software or consulting companies may not appreciate how difficult it is to get organizations to agree to share their stories; fear, risk avoidance, and lack of openness to industry collaboration usually win the day. Yet as an industry, we need to learn collectively. So although I have intentionally obscured the identities of any organizational example I've cited, I'd like to thank those organizations that have been willing to share their challenges and solutions. It takes leadership, and we all benefit from it.

For any one I may have missed, please know I am nonetheless grateful.

CHAPTER 1

A Changing
Business for a
Changing Science

THE GATHERING

It was actually a really great idea at the time: let's collect what we
know.

Around 300 B.C., the ancient library of Alexandria was created. The
largest library in existence at the time, it contained the accumulated
knowledge of hundreds of thousands of papyrus scrolls. Being located at
the port city of Alexandria, the library benefited immensely from the
international trade moving through the city's ports as ships, traders,
and merchants from around the world conducted their business and
travel. Historians today believe that in many cases travelers through
Alexandria's port were actually required to surrender any books in their
possession for a period of time so that the librarians at Alexandria could
copy the literature and add it to their growing mecca of human
knowledge. It is said that there was so much papyrus being consumed
in support of the library that parchment became a growing medium for
documents and books due to papyrus shortages.

Imagine for a moment being a researcher visiting that library for the
first time. Sitting in dusty library stacks looking around at maybe

300,000 scrolls and parchments, the thought of how to find what you were looking for must have been a little overwhelming. There was no computerized index of content here (though the Alexandrians are said to have developed some form of coding system), no guarantee that what you were looking for would be found in the stacks at all, that it would be in a language you spoke, or that you would find all of what you sought as opposed to just a portion of the knowledge. My guess is if you knew exactly what single document you were looking for, an Alexandrian librarian could have probably helped you find it. But if you were trying to gather previously disparate information together to gain insights or make a decision, those dusty stacks must have looked tall indeed.

Over 2,000 years later, the story has not changed much in the practice of medical science. We managed to upgrade from papyrus to parchment, and through federal subsidies we have incentivized people to make their parchments electronic. But most of our stacks are still tall and intimidating. Medical information isn't stored in a centralized library—it is spread out all over the world, some locations known, others hidden and locked away, unpublished, or even unknown. We don't share a common language. And we don't require people to share their knowledge—some do voluntarily, some do under extreme duress, and others simply decline. Like the researcher standing at the Alexandrian library help desk, if we know a document exists, we might be able to find someone to help us locate it. But there are no guarantees that it exists, where it might be, what condition it might be in, or how useful it might be to our purpose.

As a visitor to Alexandria, if you aren't able to read that latest sidesplitting play by Sophocles, no one experiences physical harm. If you aren't able to discover and explore the common themes in Platonic writings, entire segments of the population do not suffer. But in a world where our ability to aggregate and consume medical information has not advanced considerably over reading papyrus, lives are damaged. People suffer. Patients even die.

The good news is that other aspects of Alexandrian society—financial trade, communications, and retail—all grew up over the past twenty centuries. We now send and receive orders, remit payments, participate in individual and group dialogues, and countless other advances by structuring and standardizing data through information technology (IT). Beyond simply conducting business, we can actually analyze and improve business—our information and technology allow us to ask new questions and derive new insights about people, products, markets, behaviors, and processes. Can health care evolve to become such an insight-driven ecosystem?

HOW CAN MEDICINE BECOME SMARTER?

This book is about health analytics. It is about helping organizational leaders understand how advanced analytics can be used to improve medical outcomes, increase financial performance, deepen relationships with customers and patients, and drive new medical innovations. Beyond the theoretical, we endeavor to create a road map—a framework for how industry executives and leaders can construct an actionable plan for evolving health and life sciences through the more intelligent application of information.

Let's be honest: analytics scares some people. It sounds like you need an advanced math degree to even have a conversation about it. It can make professionals who are otherwise world-class experts in their fields a little uncomfortable. It sounds technical. And, perhaps worst of all, can you really trust statistics?

The answer, of course, is no, you absolutely cannot trust statistics . . . at least not in isolation. You cannot trust a single blood test or electrocardiogram (EKG) reading to fully diagnose and treat a patient, either. But those tests and readings provide critical information to experienced professionals who can then take actions to develop hypotheses, execute additional tests, and combine empirical and experiential data to make decisions. Analytics are no different—they combine data to offer a new source of information. And just as most physicians do not need to know how to build an EKG machine in order to use EKG readings, our goal in this book is to provide enough information about health analytics to empower nontechnical, nonmathematical industry professionals to take advantage of the tremendous promise inherent in health analytics.

Before we can talk about the opportunities, though, we need to begin to baseline where our patient—the health ecosystem—is today.

COMPLEXITY EXCEEDING COGNITION

The human brain remains the most sophisticated computing device known to humankind. With a theoretical storage capacity measured in petabytes, fully autonomous hierarchical functioning, and near-instantaneous latency to inputs, the brain is one of nature's truly greatest marvels.

And yet, this incredible device has a number of well-documented shortcomings:

1. The human mind cannot simultaneously consider more than about four pieces of information at one time. For example, consider the myriad of tradeoffs associated with buying a car: new versus used, buy versus lease, standard versus premium features, brand prestige, acquisition costs, maintenance costs, safety profile, insurance, vehicle performance, dealer incentives, customer service, fuel economy, depreciation . . . even with the power of the human brain at the ready (and accepting that people value each factor differently), is it easy for you to pick your next car? More than likely, you do what most people do to help you make this decision. They decide on a small subset of factors that are most important to them, reducing the factor count closer to four. They look to their own prior experience with cars to infer what might be best. They ask friends for recommendations, zeroing in on a single factor—consumer sentiment. And they look at periodicals like *Consumer Reports*, which reduce the complexities to "editor's choice" and ranked lists. Do physicians make decisions using a similar approach? Do executives? You bet.

2. The human mind uses undisciplined principles in weighing the importance of information. For example, the human mind places greater emphasis on the first information it receives about a topic (the primacy effect), and the most recent information it has received about a topic (called the recency effect). These principles operate regardless of whether the information is actually valuable or even accurate. Other examples of undisciplined mental principles include biases due to expectations (e.g., selective

perception, confirmation bias, contrast effect, expectation bias), inaccurate perceptions of probabilities (e.g., availability heuristic, base rate fallacy, illusory correlation, neglect of probability), the nature of the information itself (e.g., negativity bias, valence effect, bizarreness effect), and skewed perceptions of risk versus reward (pseudocertainty effect, risk compensation, loss aversion).

3. The human mind cannot easily detect its own biases. For example, people tend to read more about topics that match their interests and experiences. They also tend to associate with people who are like them. Though intuitively each one of us would agree that such biases only make sense, we are often unable to discern the degree to which these natural biases influence our ability to gather information and make decisions that might run counter to our own perspectives. If you think of everyone as viewing the world through their own particular lens, we can never fully appreciate the imperfections that might exist in our own.

These effects, among others, illustrate some of our human biological and cognitive barriers that do not preclude practicing smarter medicine, but call us to bring more discipline to the practice. In a world where decisions are made on a limited set of data and experience—when decisions are easy—it really isn't a problem. But unfortunately, the world of medicine is not such a world.

The storage and processing capacity of an individual's mind is fixed; modern analytical computing infrastructure, however, is virtually infinitely scalable. Did your research question just get twice as hard to answer? Did you just find three times the volume of information to analyze? No problem—we can just add more computers to work on the problem and still get you an answer quickly. In contrast to the limits of the human mind, there are no problems in medicine today that exceed our technology's ability to analyze data and draw conclusions. The limits are on the information we have available to us, our ability to formulate the right questions, and our determination in pursuing analytics as a disciplined lens to improving health outcomes and costs.

Throughout this book, we will explore the rising role of electronic data in understanding and improving health care. For now, let's try and frame the situation as follows:

1. The volume and complexity of health-related data (clinical, administrative, financial, behavioral, social) being generated today exceeds the capacity of the human brain to digest and draw conclusions.

2. The volume, diversity, and interdependencies in research data being generated today preclude the timely adoption of medical insights by individual medical practitioners and industry executives without the aid of analytical technology.

3. This problem of complexity is growing exponentially.

So what does this mean in practical terms? It means that the future practice of medicine is more than stethoscopes and scans. It means that clinical sciences and administration functions must become information-driven disciplines. It means that health enterprises of all types must develop new competencies in information and advanced analytics, increasingly relying on more sophisticated decision support to help optimize patient-centered care management and produce improved cost structures. In short, health and life sciences professionals of all levels must acknowledge the required use of advanced analytics to consistently make the best choices for their patients and businesses.

LEARNING FROM OTHER INDUSTRIES

There is some good news in all of this: the path ahead has already been cleared, at least in spots. If there is a silver lining in health care's cloud of lagging in its use of IT, it surely is that other industries have already figured out how to leverage information and advanced analytics to drive better performance.

One of my colleagues in the SAS Center for Health Analytics and Insights is fond of saying that her grocery store knows more about her health than her health insurer. And she is right! Think for a moment about all of the information available through grocery loyalty programs.

- What do I eat?
- Am I cost conscious (e.g., use coupons) and/or do I purchase discretionary items?
- Have I ever bought *Fitness* or *Pipes and Tobaccos* magazines?
- Do I buy more processed foods or whole foods?
- Am I brand loyal, and in what areas?
- Do I purchase a lot of over-the-counter medicines, and which ones?
- What sorts of promotions, buying incentives, and brand conversion tactics work on me?
- Which newspapers do I read (coupon codes being specific to a distribution channel)?

Retailers have experience in collecting, aggregating, analyzing, and continuously improving their business based on data. So do financial services firms who know your income, where and how often you shop, how reliable you are in paying bills, and more. Telecommunications companies know who you talk to, what types of communication you prefer (voice, chat, email, SMS), how much you use the Internet, and what tactics entice you to switch carriers.

In short, other industries have found ways of leveraging information and analytics to develop better products, improve profitability, increase customer service, and drive business performance. Those same opportunities exist in health care as well.

Consider a lady I met named Nancy.

NANCY

"Mr. Burke, this is Nancy from your bank's fraud department, how are you today?"

Up until answering this cell phone call, I was doing fine. At that particular moment, I was a little unsure.

"I'm fine, Nancy, what can I do for you?"

"Sir, we are just calling because we noticed some suspicious activity on your credit card. Are you by chance in Spain doing some gambling?"

"No, Nancy, I'm actually driving with my wife in the mountains of North Carolina." I started to add that I had a few other sins for which I could confess, but thought better of it.

"That's fine, Mr. Burke. We're calling because we noticed some unusual activity on your credit card. It appears the card information is being used by an unauthorized user, so we have deactivated the card and will send you a new one."

"Ok, Nancy. And just so I know, when did these transactions occur?"

"A few minutes ago."

Nancy was obviously on top of things, and she did a great job in saving my credit. But I knew something that Nancy probably didn't know; namely, that advanced analytics was responsible for flagging the fraudulent transaction. Even though I bought a lot of products and services online with that credit card, I knew from reading a case study on her company that sophisticated software capable of understanding my behavioral profile was able to discern that this was out of the ordinary. I don't purchase gambling services. I don't purchase overseas products and services. I don't usually make credit card purchases online during business hours. Nancy's analytics were able to do something that I used to do in a childhood game: figure out which one of these things is not like the others.

By some estimates, the health care industry loses in excess of $65 billion every year to fraud. Fraud is just one example of an analytical solution space that can be transferred from other industries to health care.

CHARACTERIZING HEALTH ANALYTICS

Health and life sciences are a rich field of opportunities for analytics. And though priorities vary across organizations and geographies (e.g., cost, safety, efficacy, timeliness, innovation, and productivity), it is worth noting that most, if not all, of the analytical capabilities needed to drive systemic changes in health care are already available in commercial software. The challenge for industry leaders should not be creating or finding the technology; rather, the challenge is linking business transformational programs to an analytical strategy:

- How can health analytics be consistently characterized and operationalized within and across organizational boundaries?
- How does anyone assess an organization's actual analytical capabilities?
- What is the relationship between a specific institution's strategy/business plan, and the corresponding implications in terms of analytical capability and capacity? What are all of the ways that analytics might help transform the business, and how can priorities be developed against those options? What are the focus areas?

In order to answer these questions, we need to start characterizing analytical opportunities. For example, most health analytics applications today can be seen to exist on a continuum between *business* analytics (e.g., cost, profitability, efficiency) and *clinical* analytics (e.g., safety, efficacy, targeted therapeutics), as depicted in Figure 1.1. All of these analytical applications are important, but those closer to the extremes are easier to manage because their scope does not cross into as many different business and information domains.

Whereas organizations have created initiatives targeting the extreme ends of the continuum (e.g., an activity-based costing initiative at a hospital), the largest challenges still reside in moving toward the middle of the continuum—linking clinical and business analytics into a more comprehensive view of health outcomes and costs. Furthermore, in order to successfully link the business and clinical perspectives, data from all

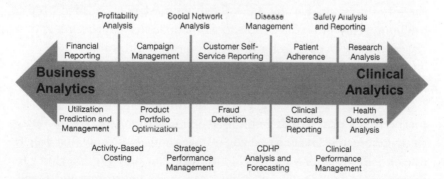

Figure 1.1 The Business-Clinical Analytics Continuum.
Source: Burke, J. (2010). "The World of Health Analytics." In *Health Informatics: Improving Efficiency and Productivity*, Ed. Stephen Kudyba, CRC Press.

three traditionally siloed markets—care providers, health plans, and researchers/manufacturers—must be joined in order to produce a more complete picture of quality, efficacy, safety, and cost. This concept—which we term *convergence*—is the topic of the next chapter. But before that, we will expand on characterizing health analytics through a device called a capability map.

THE GATHERING REVISITED

Most people who have heard of the great library at Alexandria probably also know of its tragic loss due to fire around 48 B.C. Though the exact details of the library's destruction have been somewhat obscured by history, it is clear that vast quantities of human knowledge were irrevocably lost. The *really great idea* fell victim to the most basic of risks we still face today in information management: backups.

On August 29, 2005, Hurricane Katrina made landfall in the U.S. state of Louisiana. Beyond the catastrophic losses in lives and property, an estimated one million people lost their medical information, which was stored in paper charts on racks very similar to Alexandrian library stacks. Katrina makes very tangible the impacts of our information immaturity: medical practitioners who suddenly don't know how to safely and effectively treat geographically displaced patients, and patients who— even if they were receiving optimal care before—now face suboptimal treatment plans, lost time, increased risks of complications, and disease progressions. Like our Alexandrian ancestors who walked through the ashes of once-available knowledge with what must have been a profound sense of loss, we must look at situations like Katrina with a renewed sense of passion for how to improve health care.

If your doctor handed you a bill on papyrus, what would you think? If your primary care physician whipped out a scroll and told you it was your medical chart, would you have confidence in their medical practice? If a drug researcher showed you a room filled with dusty stacks of research data and told you this was how they know that drug is safe and effective for you, would you take that pill? We are closer to these seemingly ludicrous examples than many industry professionals like to admit.

But the situation is changing.

CHAPTER 2

Convergence and the Capability Map

NICE JOB, BUT . . .

There were five of us in a circle for this team-building exercise. The youngest members were my best friend Kurt and me, both of us in our late twenties. We also had three women on the team: Amy, Terry, and Elizabeth, all of whom were mothers in their late thirties and forties. Kurt and I were both typical young men in the corporate world: energetic, passionate, and largely ignorant of all that we did not know. The three women were corporate veterans, and served as mentors to Kurt and me earlier in our careers.

The meeting facilitator must have done this exercise a thousand times, and the setup for the exercise was pretty straightforward:

> You five have crashed on a desert island. You do not know how long you will be stranded before rescue arrives—if ever. Here is a list of the specifics of your surroundings and belongings; develop a plan to survive. You have five minutes.

Enthusiastically, we jumped in to the exercise. Being so obviously experienced in such emergency situations, Kurt and I quickly started throwing out ideas, issues, and concerns. In fairness, he and I did not really dominate the five-minute exercise, but I doubt the atmosphere we created was highly collaborative . . . we were both prior Boy Scouts, we could handle this. The time elapsed quickly, and before I knew it we needed to present our plan.

Immediately on completing our presentation, the facilitator said "Nice job, but you are all dead." I don't remember exactly what we forgot that was so critical to our survival, though I recall it had nothing to do with Boy Scouts. What I do remember very clearly is looking over at Amy immediately upon hearing of our untimely demise and watching her say, "I tried to tell you a few minutes ago, but you didn't hear me."

We had beautifully illustrated what the contrived exercise was intended to show: the value of collaboration, and the results of a failure to collaborate. If I had slowed down long enough to ask, I would have learned that Amy had recently gone with her sons through a family recreational exercise that enabled her to see what I could not. And the real irony is that even though this story has stuck with me for nearly two decades as a crucial part of my own professional learning, I cannot remember what killed us. And I will never remember, because I don't have Amy's experience to frame it. The lens she brought to bear on the problem was different than mine—will always be different than mine—and you never really know when your own perspective runs short.

FIFTY FLASHLIGHTS

Now, let's imagine a new contrived situation:

> You and 49 other friends, enemies, and strangers are spontaneously transported into a giant, blackened stadium. No one can see a thing; the stadium is totally dark. You are then told that the only way out of the stadium is through a small trapdoor located in an undisclosed location. Everyone is given a tiny flashlight, but no single flashlight is bright enough to reflect the door outline . . . it allows you to see several inches in front of you, but unless you literally stumbled over the door, a person would never see it. Finally, you are told that the door is weight-activated—that it requires all 50 people to stand in the same general area of the stadium before it unlocks.

How long would it take you and your colleagues to get out of this room? How long to organize 50 people in total darkness toward a common goal? How long to form teams that create a search grid? How long to synchronize the use of flashlights so that you could see the door? How long to communicate where the door is located and bring everyone to that area of the room?

This is health care today: 20,000 black stadiums, a million tiny flashlights, and a dramatic shortage of identified doors.

CONVERGENCE DEFINED

In this book, I use the term "convergence" to describe the coming together of the many different constituents across health care toward the common goal of improving health outcomes.

Across the business of health care, convergence is producing real-world structural and business model implications. For example, some hospitals are striving to become health insurance providers, and vice versa. Similarly, the definitional lines between drug companies, medical device firms, manufacturers, contract research organizations, laboratories, biotechnology startups, and many others are blurring. In short, a complex ecosystem is restructuring, reflecting the critical need to coordinate the proverbial flashlights from our contrived exercise above.

When we talk about analytics, the concept of convergence carries some pretty important implications. For example, drug companies today are acknowledging that it doesn't make financial sense to develop drugs for which health insurers will not pay. So the historically simple question of "is it worth it to invest?" now requires insights into the world of insurers. Similarly, insurers are realizing that paying for physician-delivered services with no real understanding of what services produce good results doesn't make much business sense either. As opposed to focusing on cash flow, they should really be focusing on health flow.

In our flashlight scenario (mentioned earlier), one of the secrets to the puzzle is that individuals have to share their flashlights. If your own light isn't strong enough to find the door, you need to get help with someone else's light, and they need your light as well. Analytics provide the light, but to get it bright enough you need as many lumens as possible . . . and that comes from sharing data.

The subject of convergence could easily fill several books without ever mentioning analytics. But, suffice it to say, convergence is really composed of three distinct but completely interdependent concepts:

1. Structural changes across the health and life sciences ecosystem that are reforming what a health organization actually looks like (e.g., business models, revenue sources, changing definitions of the "customer").

2. Alignment of incentives and goals across the ecosystem that create the opportunity for getting out of our proverbial dark stadiums (e.g., agreeing to mutual success criteria such as treatment protocols, bundled payment models, shared definitions of health value).

3. Shared data and insights that open the doors of health transformation by optimizing both the strategic development of structural changes and the tactical implementation and management of aligned incentives and goals (i.e., combining flashlights to search for the doors, such as using analytics to discern what combination of services optimize health outcomes and costs).

IS CONVERGENCE REALLY REQUIRED?

Back in the early- to mid-2000s, I began arguing that convergence was required to drive the industry transformations being sought. I took on several projects, like an industry architecture initiative for the Clinical Data Interchange Standards Consortium (CDISC) that sought to establish a baseline infrastructure capable of supporting interoperability across the ecosystem, but the project outcomes were never implemented. At the time, the prevailing winds fell into three camps: convergence was too hard, there were insufficient short-term financial motivations to drive immediate action, and the internal organizational changes within individual companies and standards organizations were too political.

Fast-forward to today, and though there is tremendous variability in "how" convergence is pursued, there is not much ambiguity in "if" it is being pursued, or "what happens if we don't." But, some people may still ask, "why is this so important?" After all, if we just find better ways to cut health care costs or improve productivity, don't most of our problems go away?

Convergence is important because the nature of the questions we are asking—as scientists, care providers, business executives, even as a society—are not simple questions that can be answered using a single perspective. For example, consider for a moment the concept of care optimization. Medicine has held a long and heated debate on whether care optimization is best delivered through standardized treatments within a population of patients, or whether individualized treatments produce better, safer, more cost-effective results. Inherent in this debate is an assumption that these two worldviews—population-based or individual-based—exist on a single continuum, and that we somehow need to pick.

Today, we know that population-based and individual-based care strategies do not actually exist on the same continuum—they are actually orthogonal to each other, as depicted in Figure 2.1. Populations vary in size, complexity, and makeup. And more importantly, a given patient within a population brings unique characteristics to the table. Smart care providers discriminate on how unique the population dimension is for this particular patient. These providers also assess whether the treatment program needs to be biased toward genetic

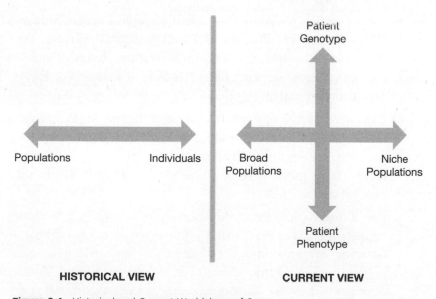

Figure 2.1 Historical and Current Worldviews of Care.

factors (i.e., the patient's genotype) versus a myriad of other factors such as behaviors and environment that could have an equal or greater impact on the patient's eventual therapeutic outcomes.

As complex as that example may seem, that analysis is a fairly simple metaphor for the plethora of information-based decisions that need to be made in our medical ecosystem today. Consider the following:

- Can a health insurer understand and predict the financial implications of an individual patient's risk of cardiovascular disease without
  a) understanding the individual's medical and behavioral profiles, and
  b) being able to readily apply the latest medical research conducted by pharmaceutical companies and medical institutions on cholesterol management to the unique characteristics of the individual?

- Can a pharmaceutical company develop a cheaper, more effective treatment for breast cancer without knowing how and why existing treatments (its own and its competitors) actually fail in the real world, and how medical costs related to treatments escalate over time?

- Can a provider recommend a patient undergo a particular invasive diagnostic procedure without understanding the actual risks, costs, and real-world expected outcomes associated with undertaking that particular procedure for patients that closely resemble this particular patient?

- Can anyone agree how much a course of therapy for a condition like knee replacement should cost without a detailed understanding of how those costs accrue—what specific costs a hospital incurs, how much it costs to develop and manufacture the medical device, etc.?

- Can a health provider and insurer know how to best facilitate changes in a patients' behaviors toward a stronger health outcome without knowing individual patients' behavioral propensities—how they like to receive information, what sorts of programs they are likely to respond, and what motivates their decision-making?

So yes, transparency and collaboration are required to transform health care, and convergence is key. It is a shame we might be doing it wrong.

THE RUSH TO HEALTH IT

With several strokes of a pen during his first term, U.S. President Barack Obama doubled the size of the health information technology (IT) market through the American Recovery and Reinvestment Act (ARRA), Patient Protection and Affordable Care Act (PPACA) and Health Information Technology for Economic and Clinical Health (HITECH) Act. Recognizing the critical importance of electronic health information and the long-standing barriers to adoption that were effectively blocking investments in IT across health care, these government-provided incentives toward electronic medical records (EMRs) and "meaningful use" did more to shift the industry toward infrastructure modernization than any single act or time period in U.S. history. Interestingly, this model of government stimulus supporting the migration to EMRs was the primary model adopted early in other countries such as the United Kingdom—countries that enjoy high EMR penetration today.

Unfortunately, this transformational agenda missed something pretty big: the difference between data and information. The long-standing dirty truth in health IT is that the EMR system does not actually capture information that can be easily consumed by either humans or computers. Many physicians dislike EMRs; they offer little help in practicing medicine, and actually inhibit it in some cases. Most technical analysts also hate EMRs; much of the medical data (e.g., physician progress notes, discharge summaries) exists in massive, unstructured buckets of text that are difficult to access, let alone analyze and derive decisions. If the medical industry had been looking for the proverbial needle, we now have them within hundreds of haystacks. And this situation won't be easily remedied; it will take a whole new generation of health software to move our data collection practices from "unstructured and ugly" to "structured and useful."

The digitization of electronic health information carried many goals, but certainly one of them was to help care providers and researchers become more data-driven. Unfortunately, if you don't know what you are going to do with data, it is impossible to collect and manage it properly. Advanced analytical software firms have thankfully developed some creative methods for dealing with the problems rampant in EMR data, but every health care executive and leader should learn a lesson from this experience: planning how you need to consume information is as important as figuring out how to collect it.

So how do we start to plan for consuming health data in new, creative, powerful ways that support the sorts of transformational ideas we are talking about? One idea is called a "capability map."

THE CAPABILITY MAP

The changes inherent in convergence are a big journey, requiring organizations to re-conceptualize what competencies are needed, how data are collected and managed, and how clinical and business decisions are made. Like any big journey, it is a good idea to establish a map and a planned route. On a health analytics map, five "continents"—areas of analytical competencies—define the major categories of analytical innovations that modern health organizations will need:

1. **Clinical and Health Outcomes Analytics.** These analytics are related to maximizing the use of existing treatments and therapies. For example, providers and health plans are both driven to ensure the best treatment is pursued for a particular patient, not just patients in general. Patient safety, health, and wellness analytics fall into this category as well.

2. **Research and Development Analytics.** These analytics are related to discovering, researching, and developing novel treatments and therapies. For example, pharmaceutical researchers and providers need to know where potential clinical trial participants can be located in order to expedite new drug development.

3. **Commercialization Analytics.** These analytics are related to maximizing sales, marketing, and customer relationship efforts. For example, both providers and health plans are motivated to communicate more frequently and effectively with patients regarding products, services, and treatments.

4. **Finance and Fraud Analytics.** These analytics, which could be considered part of Business Operations (see continent 5), relate to ensuring the financial health and stability of the organization. They are called out separately here due to the strategic role that claims, fraud, and risk play within health care markets.

5. **Business Operations Analytics.** These analytics are related to driving productivity, profitability, and compliance across the various business functions of an institution. For example, health plans and pharmaceutical manufacturers are motivated to ensure optimal operation of call center facilities, staff, and assets.

Notice that these five continents are not dependent on whether an organization is a provider, payer, pharmaceutical, biotechnology, government, or any other specific type of health organization. Despite differing market structures, business models, and incentives, most health care organizations have similar analytical needs: how to identify the best treatments, how to operate more profitably, how to engage customers more effectively, etc. Though the motivations behind undertaking analytical initiatives may vary, the analyses, their corresponding data, and even the analytical models and software that produce the results are comparable.

Within each of our five health analytics continents, a growing catalog of analytical competencies exists, as depicted in Figure 2.2. Each box represents a class of analytics-driven capabilities that provide critical insights into surviving and thriving in a converged health ecosystem.

Throughout this book, we propose specific analytical innovations aligned to this taxonomy. In thinking about how analytically-derived innovation maps to your own institution, you may identify additional boxes for the capability map. You may determine that you disagree with a definition of a box we have provided. You may also find that it is difficult to figure out on which continent a specific box should rightly reside. All of these outcomes are ok—the map's primary role is as a planning tool. If it serves to document your health analytics world map and route, it has performed its job.

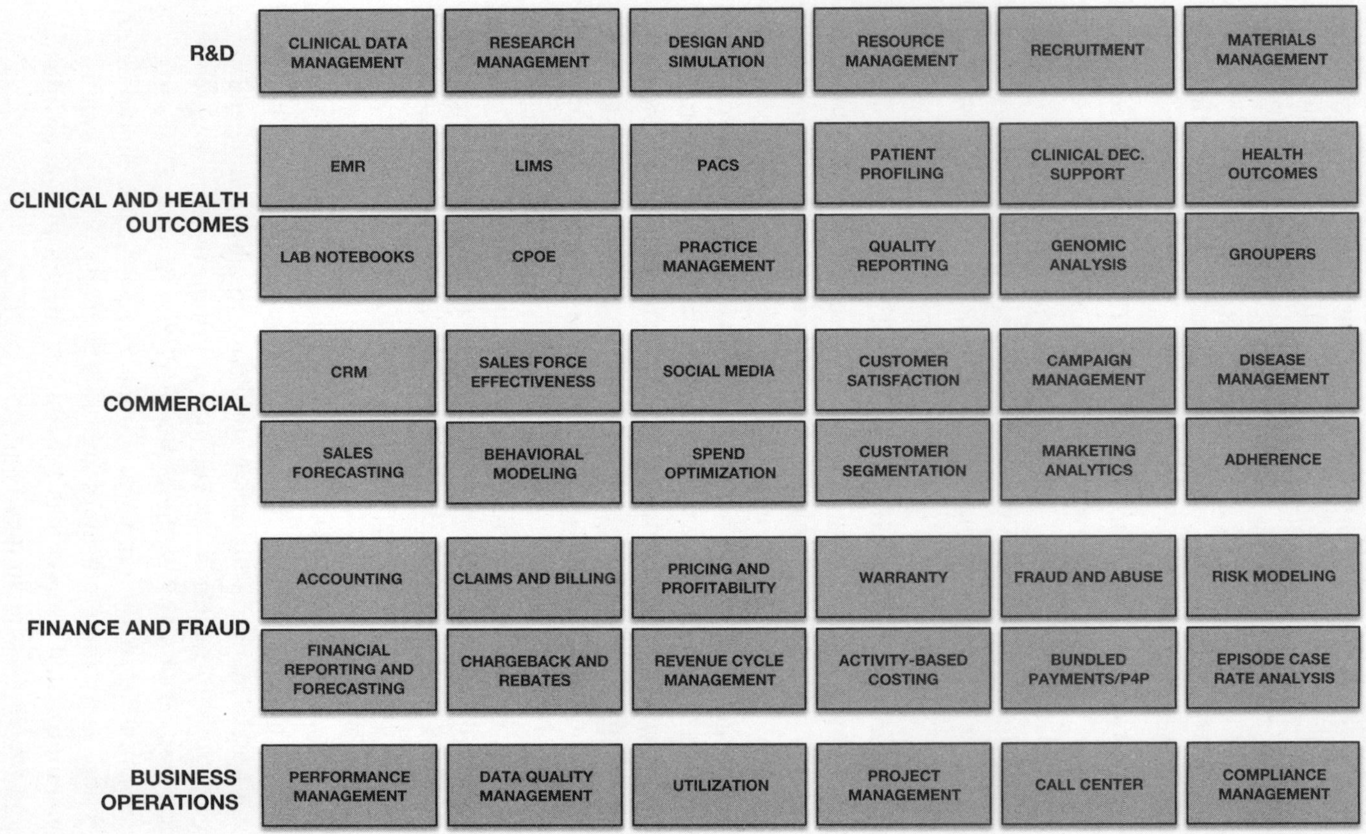

R&D

CLINICAL DATA MANAGEMENT	RESEARCH MANAGEMENT	DESIGN AND SIMULATION	RESOURCE MANAGEMENT	RECRUITMENT	MATERIALS MANAGEMENT

CLINICAL AND HEALTH OUTCOMES

EMR	LIMS	PACS	PATIENT PROFILING	CLINICAL DEC. SUPPORT	HEALTH OUTCOMES
LAB NOTEBOOKS	CPOE	PRACTICE MANAGEMENT	QUALITY REPORTING	GENOMIC ANALYSIS	GROUPERS

COMMERCIAL

CRM	SALES FORCE EFFECTIVENESS	SOCIAL MEDIA	CUSTOMER SATISFACTION	CAMPAIGN MANAGEMENT	DISEASE MANAGEMENT
SALES FORECASTING	BEHAVIORAL MODELING	SPEND OPTIMIZATION	CUSTOMER SEGMENTATION	MARKETING ANALYTICS	ADHERENCE

FINANCE AND FRAUD

ACCOUNTING	CLAIMS AND BILLING	PRICING AND PROFITABILITY	WARRANTY	FRAUD AND ABUSE	RISK MODELING
FINANCIAL REPORTING AND FORECASTING	CHARGEBACK AND REBATES	REVENUE CYCLE MANAGEMENT	ACTIVITY-BASED COSTING	BUNDLED PAYMENTS/P4P	EPISODE CASE RATE ANALYSIS

BUSINESS OPERATIONS

PERFORMANCE MANAGEMENT	DATA QUALITY MANAGEMENT	UTILIZATION	PROJECT MANAGEMENT	CALL CENTER	COMPLIANCE MANAGEMENT

Figure 2.2 Example of an Analytical Capability Map.

PUTTING THE CAPABILITY MAP TO USE

So once you develop an analytical capabilities map, how do you put it to use? There are a number of different ways organizations can use a taxonomy such as the one mentioned earlier:

1. **Linking to Business Strategy and Plan.** How will the organization compete? What are the business objectives and priorities over the next 12–18 months? Many strategic planning frameworks[1] can be highly complementary with the taxonomy in formulating business transformation initiatives.

2. **Maturity Assessment.** How well is the organization positioned to deliver against each analytical need described? Analytical competencies represent an evolutionary capability (see Figure 2.3) starting with basic reporting, advancing through more sophisticated types of statistical methods, and eventually reaching predictive modeling and optimization. Thus, understanding where an organization's competencies currently reside

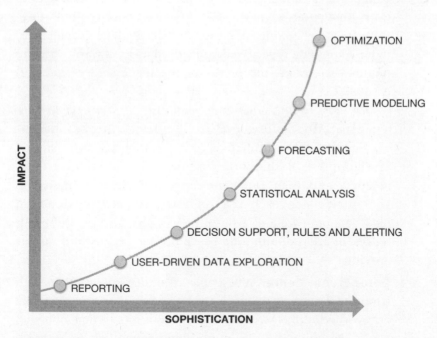

Figure 2.3 Analytical Maturity Model.

along each of the capability map's dimensions is instructive in organizational development planning.

3. **Staffing.** For any organization to deliver against any single analytical scenario, three types of human resources are needed. First, an industry expert in the specific business question of interest is needed to guide the approach to answering the question. Second, an analytical expert is needed to construct the statistical methods to be used to answer the question. And third, a technologist is needed to manage the use of analytical software and applications in support of the business. Organizations must ensure all three of these needs are being met in order to ensure the accuracy, repeatability, and ultimate success of any analytical initiatives.[2]

4. **Infrastructure Planning.** Does the organization have all of the IT assets—data, analytical software, scalable computing capacity—required to fully address the need? Data issues—in particular, data integration, standardization, quality management, enhancement, and governance—are tremendous challenges to every analytical scenario. And whereas existing "reporting" software may be sufficient for lower-level analytical capabilities, more computing capacity and advanced analytical software are required to unlock the power of the higher-order analytical capabilities.

   The first four issues—understanding the strategy, competency maturity, staffing levels, and infrastructure readiness—can be inked into a unified planning framework as illustrated in Figure 2.4. Each column represents an analytical competency, and each row represents a readiness dimension. The numbers in each cell represent subjectively reported readiness on a scale of 1 (low) to 5 (high), and the bold cells represent areas of attention based on the priority and ratings provided.

5. **Competency Center.** A best practice among organizations with strong analytical capabilities is the formation of an organizational entity specifically accountable for institutionalizing analytics across the enterprise. Far more than an internal "help desk,"

CLINICAL MANAGEMENT	CLINICAL DEC. SUPPORT	QUALITY REPORTING	GENOMIC ANALYSIS	HEALTH OUTCOMES
PRIORITY	MEDIUM	HIGH	LOW	MEDIUM
MATURITY	1	4	1	2
STAFFING—SUBJECT MATTER	3	5	4	5
STAFFING—ANALYTICAL	4	4	1	2
STAFFING—TECHNICAL	4	4	4	3
READINESS—DATA	2	5	1	2
READINESS—SOFTWARE	4	5	1	1
READINESS—COMPUTING CAPACITY	2	3	3	4

Figure 2.4 An Example of a Unified Planning Framework.

these competency centers provide internal consulting and mentoring related to

- business plan execution and maturity oversight (e.g., issues #1 and #2)
- statistical methodologies
- data management
- centralized computational resource management and capacity planning
- analytical/data asset reusability
- ongoing refinement of the taxonomy
- aspects of governance (e.g., enterprise data strategy)

HEALTH ANALYTICS AS A DISCIPLINE

What does a 21st-century health care environment look like? In many ways, it remains to be defined. But it certainly is an environment much more heavily focused on cost, quality, safety, and outcomes than the 20th-century environment. It is also an environment that should be grounded in new incentive models that tear down the rampant silos in health care in favor of high quality, cross-continuum coordinated patient care. The ability to provide that focus is completely dependent on an ability to articulate and understand the clinical and business implications of the patients we see, the treatments we provide, and the processes we use to deliver it all. And regardless of where any particular organization or institution is today on the path towards analytical maturity, a solid and growing health analytics strategy will be crucial to success.

Ultimately, each organization will develop its own map and planned route(s), differing in:

- **What is included in the analytical capability map?** The list of analytical possibilities is quite large if not endless, and organizations may uncover opportunities for innovation in pursuing analytical scenarios not represented in the figure above. The two most important aspects of building the map are: a) accurately reflecting the needs of the organization, and b) reflecting those needs in a way that is generalizable to more than one market so that discussions around shared data and analytical models can proceed unimpaired.

- **Where do certain analytical needs sit within the capability map?** Should "Bending the Cost Curve" (a colloquialism regarding restructuring clinical and administrative cost models to reflect a post-reform U.S. business climate) be in the "Business Operations" or "Finance and Fraud" domain? In the end, it probably doesn't matter as long as the needs are represented.

- **How do the relative priorities rank within the map?** Organizations may competitively differentiate themselves based on business strategies that imply differing priorities across the various analytical scenarios. Alternatively, their business models may naturally reflect a bias toward certain analytics. These priorities may differ by functional business unit within an organization as well.

In the final analysis, convergence and our map lead us to an unavoidable conclusion: health transformation will be fueled by insights that optimize clinical, financial, and individual patient perspectives. Trying to optimize clinical outcomes regardless of costs and individual differences is not possible. Catering to the needs of individual patients regardless of clinical or financial implications cannot serve the needs of a sustainable, affordable, and effective health ecosystem.

Though our map defines analytical domains discretely, the real win is in understanding the interdependencies between the five major health analytics continents. Just as tectonic shifts of one continent on Earth have unavoidable effects on other continents, so our analytical efforts must identify, respect, predict, and optimize the relationships between clinical, financial, and personal concerns.

NOTES

1. For example, Kaplan, R. and Norton, D. (2004). *Strategy Maps: Converting Intangible Assets into Tangible Outcomes*, Harvard Business Press.
2. These three resources may not be distinct individuals, but it is uncommon to find all three in the same individual at a high level of quality and depth.

CHAPTER 3

The Four Enterprise Disciplines of Health Analytics

HERESY

When the great museum and library at Alexandria was being developed, the science of medicine as we know it was just beginning. At the time, the Greek deity, Asclepius, was considered the god of medicine, and his serpent-bound staff is still found in our medical symbols today. The followers of Asclepius were a popular and growing movement, and the cult built healing temples called asclepeions across the empire to provide for those with medical needs.

One of the more famous asclepeions of the time was located on the Greek island of Kos. Interestingly, Kos also held a provincial branch of the Alexandrian museum, and as a result became a leading seat of education in the region. And around 460 B.C. on this island, a man named Hippocrates was born and educated.

For the next several hundred years, this tiny island—around 125 square miles—represented an interesting convergence of three disciplines: science, religion, and education. The foundations of modern medicine can be traced to the people and knowledge at Alexandria and Kos. And as the new science developed, we are left to wonder to what degree the followers of Asclepius may have considered the new discipline of medicine to be heresy.

In this chapter, we attempt to do what some may consider heretical: reduce the complexities of health analytics down into a brief synopsis that any business leader needs to know in order to drive an analytics-powered business strategy. In doing so, we run the risk of offending the die-hard, true-to-the-core statisticians, technologists, and academicians who will rightly claim that fundamental concepts are being missed. But the goal of this book is not to create new analytical experts—the goal is to create leaders capable of building analytically driven organizations (which will, by necessity, include those same experts).

In pursuing that goal, we first need to dispel a myth: real analytics is not about reporting. Whether through over-marketing or under-educating, many executives today believe that the foundation of an advanced analytics strategy is based on Web reports, business intelligence software, linked spreadsheets, or the "reports" tab of their favorite software. Nothing could be further from the truth.

Analytics—real analytics—is a rich discipline. Comparing analytics to business intelligence or reporting is somewhat akin to saying that a four-course meal at a five-star restaurant is defined by the side dish of potatoes. Sure, side dishes are important. But you don't take on a meal like that—putting on nice clothes, blocking out a couple of hours, enjoying the savory sensations of great foods and fine wines, a peaceful ambience—just to eat potatoes, no matter how great the potatoes. If you are not taking in the whole four-course experience, then the time, effort, and cost don't make sense.

Likewise, analytics touch a broad base of competencies covering data, mathematics, computer science, performance management, financial analysis, institutional governance, organizational culture, strategy formulation, and executive decision-making. If you like mysteries, analytics offer an endless well of questions to ask and answers to seek. If you like innovations, analytics provide a workbench whereby your imagination, creativity, and business acumen can unlock a wellspring of new business strategies, product offerings, and services. If you like science or history or even magic tricks, analytics give a microscope for understanding the past, a discipline for understanding why things are the way they are today, and a crystal ball for predicting the future. There really is something here for everyone.

But the insights are not found on a reports tab.

HEALTH ANALYTICS FOR THE NONANALYTICAL

Health analytics involve competencies in four foundational and inter-related disciplines:

1. **Information Management**—aggregating, standardizing, restructure, and preparing the rising quantities of data for analysis.

2. **Statistics**—applying mathematical principles to available data in order to describe the past, understand the present, and predict the future.

3. **Information Delivery**—making analytical results and software assets available to individuals responsible for making decisions and taking actions.

4. **High-Performance Computing**—reducing the time required to conduct analyses and surface information by leveraging advanced technology infrastructure.

Though some people choose to focus analytics discussions on the statistics discipline, from organizational and leadership perspectives, each of these four disciplines is critically important. A weak information management strategy produces a garbage-in/garbage-out problem, where people cannot trust what the analytics produce. A weak statistics strategy—one that focuses on understanding the past without predicting the future or optimizing the present—creates an environment where the advanced analytics return on investment is questionable. An information delivery strategy that only makes analytical results available to a handful of analysts and executives lacks the scale needed to produce meaningful business change. And an insufficient high-performance computing environment may mean that people need to wait weeks to get the insights needed for today's decisions.

In the following sections, we will explore each of these four disciplines: what they are, how they are interrelated, and how industry leaders should think about their development.

INFORMATION MANAGEMENT

By our estimates, around 60% of the time and 40% of the costs associated with doing analytical solutions are attributable purely to data: what is it? where is it? how good is it? is there enough of it? is it ready for analysis? can it answer the questions we are asking? how can we supplement it?, etc. It is ironic that executives can be intimidated by the math of advanced analytics; the people who actually do the work are usually happy to get to the math stage of a project. And the challenges are often never even visible to leaders.

I asked Candice, a biostatistician at a pharmaceutical company, how much of her time was actually related to performing statistics of some kind.

"That's one of the most frustrating things for my team," she said. "In my team, we've estimated that we only spend about 10% of our time using our statistical training."

"Why is that?", I asked.

"It's the data," she said. "For every project we work on, we spend over 75% of our time moving data around. By the time we get finished working with the data—getting access to it, understanding what is in it, restructuring it for analysis, and a bunch of other things—we have very little time to focus on the real statistics."

Having worked with hundreds of biostatisticians, I can tell you that Candice's experience is far from unique. We use the term *data* a lot here, but this topic is really about the more comprehensive competencies within information management. And with the growing volumes and complexities of health-related information, these competencies are becoming mission critical.

As illustrated in Figure 3.1, we believe there are seven vectors to a modern information management strategy supporting health analytics.

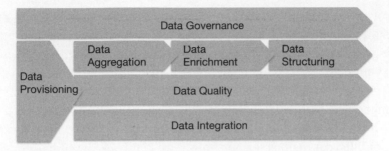

Figure 3.1 The Seven Vectors of Information Management.

1. **Data Governance**—the enterprise-wide management process by which strategies, policies, and decisions related to data are made.

2. **Data Provisioning**—the process of acquiring new sources of data from beyond an organization's walls.

3. **Data Aggregation**—the process of bringing together data from disparate data sources that may be analytically useful.

4. **Data Enrichment**—the process of improving and extending the representation of data within a repository in anticipation of how the information will be analyzed.

5. **Data Structuring**—the process of creating and managing analyzable data assets.

6. **Data Quality**—improving the reliability and accuracy of data, feeding both operational systems and analytical programs.

7. **Data Integration**—the technical processes and tools used to access all applicable sources of data.

Setting aside for a moment the somewhat technical nature of this topic, one way to think about information management is in terms of outfitting a new home with plumbing. The first thing you need in order to have a nice home with water in the right places is a set of needs from the buyer and a blueprint for the plumbing—and that is what data governance provides. You are also going to need a source for the water, usually either municipal water or a well, and that is what data provisioning sets up. Next, you will need a lot of physical pipes and hoses— the data integration portion of our model. And based on what you know about water contamination in the area (we are building this health analytics home in an obviously underdeveloped country), you are going to need some water purifiers and filters (data quality). Based on your plans, you are probably going to need some bathtubs and sinks (data aggregation and data structuring), and the ability to control temperature with separate hot and cold faucets and a hot water heater (data enrichment). The successful execution of the preceding unlocks a lot of different options for our house: we can cook, wash hands, take showers, water the lawn, and many other tasks. And missing any one of these competencies dramatically lowers the value of our house (e.g., cold showers, unfit drinking water).

Information management is a huge domain. Table 3.1 highlights some of the key implications leaders need to consider in taking on the development of these competencies.

CASE STUDY

Does Information Management Really Pay Off?

Can investing in better enterprise information management capabilities actually have a measurable impact on productivity?

In one case, an East Coast nonprofit health plan was processing more than 100 million member claims a year. Due to the volume of data and the increasing number of source data providers, the actuarial team was routinely devoting 70–80% of its time preparing data for analysis. One leader commented, "Our time should be spent performing the types of analyses that help us manage risk better for our members and our plan." Yet the data work was so significant that individual analysts were developing data management specializations as opposed to analytical specializations and insights.

The organization initiated an internal project focused on developing a modernized approach to just three of the seven information management vectors: data integration, data aggregation, and data structuring. The results? The time analysts were spending in non-value-added data tasks was cut by more than 50%, and the time to data availability improved by up to 70%.

"We can now spend the bulk of our time investigating trends and determining if outcomes are aligned with expectations and corporate strategy."

Table 3.1 Information Management Issues and Implications

Topic	Why Is It Important?	Implications
Data governance	The unplanned growth and management of information dramatically escalates costs and reduces analytical efficacy	▪ Organizational divisions and departments will need to begin talking and undertaking shared accountability for information asset development, management, and maintenance ▪ Business and technology representation is needed in this function ▪ This is not a project; it is an ongoing organizational management need
Data provisioning	Health organizations of all sizes and types need to begin incorporating data from beyond their organizational walls	▪ Data governance needs to include identifying needed third party data assets ▪ Legal resources need to be on standby for contracting, negotiations, and risk management ▪ Information technology people and infrastructure need to be in place, including adequate protections for protected health information from third parties
Data integration	Time, effort, and timeliness in accessing and pulling data escalate costs and timelines associated with delivering analytical results. Timeliness of data constrains utility of analytics	▪ Developing enterprise-wide strategies for accessing and pulling information together (shared pipes) is the gift that keeps on giving ▪ Some systems won't be ready to participate in "real time" data exchanges; "some time" is better than "no time"
Data quality	Regardless of perception, most enterprise data is of poor quality	▪ Analytical outputs are only as good as analytical inputs ▪ Technical solutions are available, but data governance will need to establish this as a priority and deal with the unavoidable policy decisions
Data aggregation	Data sources, size, and complexity are expanding faster than any organization's ability to put it all in one place	▪ Focusing on data warehouses misses the point; speed, flexibility, and extensibility are needed in data strategies

(continued)

Table 3.1 (*Continued*)

Topic	Why Is It Important?	Implications
Data enrichment	The data you have is never enough—incomplete, inconsistent, translations required	▪ Data enrichment is largely a technical function, but can be enhanced greatly through data governance ▪ Clever innovations become possible when moving data enrichment activities from simple translation exercises (e.g., ICD coding consistency) towards analytical methods being used to profile and enhance the data itself prior to analyzing the specific question at hand
Data structuring	Virtually no existing data repository is well structured for analysis, and some are not structured at all	▪ The technical process of deciding how to structure data for specific analysis is straightforward ▪ Analytical data structure development and management can be managed through a central sourcing model in order to control the natural exponential growth . . . but it requires an internal partnership model (not an ivory tower) ▪ Making analyses (and therefore their data structures) reusable is harder, and should be a longer-term goal clarified through accumulated experience

The Fourth Dimension (Time)

One of the questions that is often at the top of the mind among health leaders undertaking analytical projects is, "Why is it so hard to bring data together for this?" The answer is that, technically, it is often not hard to bring data together. What is often very hard, though, is bringing the data together in a way that supports answering health questions, because the questions often require the incorporation of time as a variable.

Health is a time-dependent domain. In order to understand health—its costs, behaviors, or outcomes—you must analyze information using a dimension of time. For example, consider for a moment that you want to understand whether this year's flu shot was effective at preventing outbreaks of the illness. If you could open up an entire electronic medical records (EMRs) database for a geographical region, you might be able to search for and isolate all of the patients that received that particular inoculation. You could then search and find the subset of those patients that subsequently contracted influenza, and compare their incidence rate to patients that had not received the inoculation.

But what is the time window you are going to use? Is it patients that received the inoculation within the past 6 months? The past year? Is the incidence rate measured for patients that contracted the disease within 3 months? Six months? A year? And how do you handle patients who contracted influenza before receiving the inoculation? How far ahead of the inoculation in time will you set the rule?

This example is easy compared to trying to understand treatment efficacy for complex, chronic, and/or comorbid diseases such as cancer, diabetes, and cardiovascular disease. The exercise is not one of counting— it is about sequencing clinical, administrative, financial, and behavioral events and measurements in such a way that meaningful questions can be asked and answered. And, of course, analyses like this depend on having access to longitudinal patient data (data covering many years of a given patient's life)—no small feat in a fragmented health ecosystem. The information management discipline allows an organization to begin to assemble longitudinal data in a scalable, repeatable, semantically consistent and business-aligned manner . . . but it is not easy.

Keeping It Real

Time is not the only consideration that has to be addressed in an information management approach supporting health analytics. The answers we uncover via analytics are constrained by:

- Validity—how appropriate is the measuring instrument in reflecting the phenomenon you wish to observe? For example, a medical claims record is not a valid instrument for inferring disease state. Medical practices, motivated to file claims that actually get paid, do not focus their claims data entry on clinical accuracy; rather, they focus on claims processing efficiency and effectiveness. So claims data is a reasonably invalid indicator of underlying medical disease, but an excellent indicator of reimbursement distribution. Validity includes the concept of resolution—is the instrument measuring the detail of the phenomenon you intend to observe?

- **Reliability.** How consistently does the observational instrument report the phenomenon under observation? For example, a health insurer is often a highly reliable source for reimbursable medical expenses—if a patient receives the care, they get the transaction. But only part of the year's data is reliable—once a patient hits a spending ceiling for a procedure (for example, ten chiropractor visits), they often stop filing claims since the claims won't be paid anyway. So claims data may reliably describe reimbursable health utilization, but not actual health utilization.

When working properly, organizational leaders should expect that priorities and decisions around data governance, provisioning, quality, and enrichment will be influenced heavily by analytical experts communicating the limits of reliability and validity associated with existing information assets.

STATISTICS

Most health industry leaders deal with statistics in one form or another everyday. Whether in scientific journals, business reports, or consumer publications, people are regularly confronted with statistical concepts. Most of these encounters deal with what are called descriptive statistics—mathematical summarizations of existing data. For example, readmission rates in hospitals are descriptive statistics—they summarize a group of patients' history over a period of time. Retail spending was up last quarter; electorate polling shows candidate A is favored over candidate B; the clinic was less profitable last quarter; consumers are spending more time on the Internet. All of these are examples of how people use descriptive statistics.

Descriptive statistics are very useful for doing exactly what their name implies—describing things, answering "what" types of questions. They are much less useful for answering why or how questions. For those questions, you need inferential statistics, which empower us to explore the relationships between concepts and draw inferences from what we observe. Through inferential statistics, we can test hypotheses, detect correlations between otherwise unrelated entities, and extrapolate beyond our observable data to the unobserved. We can discover hidden patterns in data through data mining, and build predictive models for how to optimize a set of desirable outcomes.

Statistical inference is a key component of the scientific method, so inferential statistics are crucial to drawing conclusions from medical research. But they are also pivotal in nonscientific applications as well. Forecasting, for example, models a pattern in observable data to predict likely future financial outcomes. Data mining allows us to detect, measure, and model consumer sentiment in social media. Statistical modeling allows us to detect and prevent claims fraud. So inferential statistics are just as important to nonscientific analyses as they are to scientific ones.

In terms of software, descriptive statistics are all over the place. Most enterprise-level software applications include the ability to generate reports that count, group, average, and calculate percentages on the data within the system. For the better part of two decades, business intelligence and reporting software has offered dedicated software platforms for aggregating and summarizing data using an inventory of descriptive statistical formulas. Easily, the most pervasive descriptive statistical tool used around the world today is Microsoft Excel.

In contrast, inferential statistics are much less pervasive. One reason is that inferential statistics usually require a deeper technical skill set on the part of the end user in order to exercise the software. They also usually require the end user to really understand statistical theory and methods as a mathematical discipline; otherwise, misapplication and misinterpretation can produce seriously flawed results and interpretations. In recent years, clever software designers have built smarter, easier-to-use, and more self-guiding software that have reduced many of these barriers. These innovations have opened the door for the broader use of statistics across organizations and users. But there should be no confusion that statistical training is usually required in order to properly exercise and exploit inferential statistical techniques.

The language of statistics is expansive, specialized, and beyond the scope of this book. Nevertheless, it is useful for industry leaders to have a frame of reference for some of the concepts presented within the domain of statistics. Table 3.2 summarizes some of the more important, commonly used terms and concepts found in health analytics.

Without going further into the complexities of when and how to deploy the actual analytics, the two takeaways for industry leaders are 1) these capabilities are available in commercial software today,

Table 3.2 Statistical Concepts and Terms

Concept	Definition
Models	An overly generalized term used to describe either analytical structures (i.e., how mathematical relationships and assumptions are defined) or data structures (i.e., how data are designed and rendered).
Predictive Analytics	A collection of inferential statistical processes and methods used to predict the probability of a particular outcome. Often used interchangeably with the term "predictive modeling."
Scoring	The process of applying a predictive model to data sets. The score applied is often the propensity towards a particular outcome or behavior. For example, the predictive modeling process of financial credit scoring scores a person on creditworthiness.
Forecasting	A collection of techniques used in predictive analytics for estimation and prediction, usually incorporating time as a dimension for analysis.
Descriptive Modeling	A collection of techniques used in predictive analytics to infer groupings, categories, and multidimensional relationships within data. For example, descriptive modeling can be used to segment customers based on multiple emergent characteristics such as age, buying patterns, and education.
Data mining	A collection of statistical and computer science techniques used to discover patterns in oftentimes large data sets. Includes the discipline of "text mining," which applies data mining techniques to unstructured textual data for purposes of detecting patterns and deriving structures.
Optimization	More formally called "operations research," optimization is a collection of inferential statistical and computer science techniques applied to maximize decisions and outcomes for complex problems and models.
Simulation	A term used to describe applying statistical models to imitate the real world usually for the purposes of better understanding how the real world works.
Data Visualization	A term used to describe both the discipline of and software for illustrating data graphically. Data visualization software can cover both descriptive and inferential statistics.

and 2) talented people know how and when to apply them when they see clear goals and objectives.

INFORMATION DELIVERY

Health analytics offer absolutely no value if people cannot fit the analytics into their professional lives. Beyond the specialists often responsible for information management and statistics, there are three activities that unlock the value of health analytics for health professionals:

1. Viewing the results of analytical scenarios
2. Manipulating analytical models to gain additional insights
3. Taking actions and making decisions based on analytical insights

The ways in which users can and should participate in each of these activities varies widely by user type, analytical scenario, and business process. But generally speaking, these activities are supported by three different information delivery paradigms.

1. **Desktop Applications.** The foundation of any successful analytical project is the analytical application itself. We're using the term application to describe the software people are using to: a) exercise the analytical capabilities (e.g., do this analysis), and b) provide the results to the end user (i.e., show me the table, listing, graph, etc.). Many analytical applications today are delivered via Web pages or portals, though some more sophisticated types of interactions still lend themselves to dedicated software installs. The important point for leaders to understand is that whatever techniques and tools are used, if the information delivery model does not fit with the way individuals work, the intended business results will not be achieved. So it is very important to focus not just on "What is the question we want to answer?" but also, "What are we going to do with the information . . . how are we planning to use this analysis?"

2. **Mobile Applications.** If health care is anything, it is mobile. When shadowing some health practitioners on an oncology ward one day, I asked a nurse at the nursing station how she mainly

used the computer on the counter. She looked at me and kindly asked, "When would I be here to use a computer?" Her point was that desk jobs don't really exist when dealing with patient care. The dramatic proliferation of smartphones and tablet computing devices seen across the health ecosystem today is a testament to the simple truth that the most meaningful information people have is the information at their fingertips in front of the patient, during the consult, in the lunch room, and on the elevator. If you really want analytical insights to power your enterprise—if you really want analytics to stick—a mobility strategy is a good idea.

3. **Real-Time Integration.** Perhaps the most potent yet under-represented way of incorporating health analytics into modern business is through surfacing analytics within other enterprise business processes and software systems. We will probably always need dedicated desktop and mobile analytics applications as well, but if you really want to impact how people are doing their jobs, go through the systems in which they are performing those jobs—the EMRs, practice management systems (PMSs), claims, billing, clinical trials, and myriad other software systems where users already work. "Inject" the analytical insights into the business processes themselves, and you've found a way to increase information-based decisions without dramatically changing the way people work.

All three of the information delivery paradigms—desktop applications, mobile applications, and real-time integration—are important to building an analytically driven health enterprise. Indeed, the same analytical business capability might be deployed through all three paradigms within a given institution at the same time. For example, analysts might build out a desktop application that models patient health risks using both clinical and nonclinical sources of data. A mobile application on the iPad might use the same risk models to prompt a nurse practitioner to ask some further probing questions during a high-risk patient interview. It might also be a service called by other software to implement a new disease management campaign targeting high-risk patients of a particular profile. As the analytical models improve over time, all three uses can benefit from the same investment.

HIGH-PERFORMANCE COMPUTING

As competencies with information management and analytics increase, leaders rapidly begin to realize the power in using information to drive business decisions. At that point, two things inevitably happen: the number of questions asked increases, and the complexity of each question increases. Volume and complexity both carry performance demands on an organization's information technology (IT) resources, so it is best to plan in advance how to manage the growing demands being placed on its analytical infrastructure.

Generally speaking, there are three ways to manage the changing business demands on IT processing speed and capacity:

1. **Scale Up**—the ability to increase the performance of existing physical computing resources: faster CPUs, more memory, more storage, or more CPU cycles. Virtualization—partitioning and dynamically re-allocating large computing assets according to the functional demands of the business—is one technique IT organizations are using to manage scale up needs while still achieving reasonable economies of scale.

2. **Scale Out**—the ability to allocate additional physical computing resources on demand: add more computers, for example, or redistribute work across a broader set of computers. Cloud computing and grid computing are two models used today to manage scale out needs. Newer computing architectures such as Apache Hadoop are also examples of scale-out designs.

3. **Scale In**—deconstructing computing tasks into smaller, discrete units that can be redeployed into specialized performance environments. In-database computing (i.e., when analytical algorithms run within a database) and appliance-based computing (i.e., dedicated hardware optimized to perform only specialized tasks) are examples of scale-in solutions.

All of the above high-performance models are proven approaches, and most organizations need some combination of all three in order to effectively manage their evolving business needs.

MATURATION AND SCALE

In Chapter 2, we briefly introduced the concept of an analytical maturity model—the idea that organizations grow in their analytical capabilities over time. Basic capabilities such as reporting and alerting can evolve into more powerful and sophisticated forms of advanced analytics.

As Figure 3.2 illustrates, the progression of maturity is not necessarily linear or sequential; organizations can pursue multiple levels of sophistication at the same time, though major jumps across the continuum are progressively more difficult to operationalize. More importantly, though, maturity is specific to the capability map taxonomy area or domain. For example, an organization that is adept at predictive modeling of customer responses does not necessarily have capabilities in predictive modeling of health outcomes (see Figure 3.3). Though the statistical concepts are the same, there are many differences: the formulation of good questions, the discovery of limitations, the specific data assets, the knowledge from prior work, experience in managing advanced analytical projects, etc.

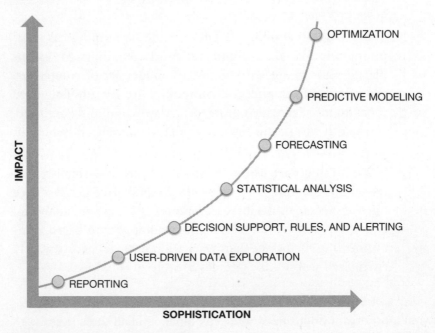

Figure 3.2 Analytical Maturity Model.

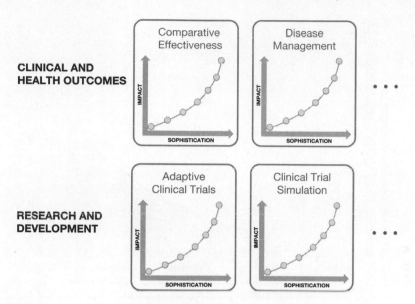

Figure 3.3 Capability Maturity is Domain Specific.

In hearing this, some leaders question the wisdom, viability, and benefit of a centralized analytical services function within their organizations. If analytical competency is capability domain-specific, should a company expect to derive benefits of scale from a shared services resourcing model? In our experience, the answer is overwhelmingly yes. Though a given line of analytical inquiry matures independently, the benefits of a dedicated competency center outlined in Chapter 2 nonetheless hold true.

There is one other aspect of maturity and scale that we need to point out: the actual analytical models should mature over time as well. And this is where tremendous power becomes unlocked. When some leaders think about health analytics, prior experiences with basic reporting and business intelligence come to mind: the benefit of a given report is basically delivered when the report is finalized.

As shown in Figure 3.4, that is not true in advanced analytics. Advanced analytical models should be organic; they can grow and improve over time. Models get fine-tuned over time to better represent the question and the real world. New data sources can be added that improve the validity, reliability, and precision of the model. New

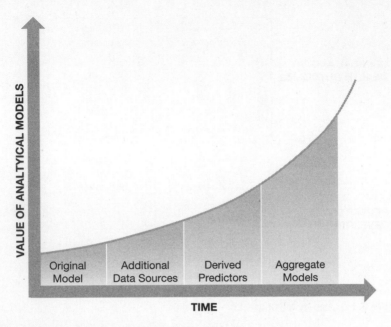

Figure 3.4 Growing Returns of Analytical Investments.

predictive factors can be derived from data. Models can even be combined together. As the strength of any analytical model grows, the business opportunity, value, and return on investment associated with that model grow as well.

ENTERPRISE-CLASS ANALYTICS: PUTTING IT ALL TOGETHER

By now, it is probably becoming apparent that health analytics are more than a project. A winning strategy for health analytics is a lot more complex than simply picking some statistical software and hiring a few analysts. The disciplines of information management, statistics, information delivery, and high-performance computing represent enterprise-level commitments. Organizations need to attain or expand certain business and technical abilities in order to successfully unlock the value of health analytics:

- Business leaders must tackle the realities of enterprise-wide information governance and sharing, new competency development, resourcing (including in-house vs. outsourced), shared services models, shifting business processes closer to real time, and compliance and privacy protections that satisfy the business and regulatory needs without stifling innovation.

- IT professionals accountable for an enterprise-class health analytics strategy need to be focused on enabling and delivering core enterprise architecture abilities: scalability, availability, manageability, reliability, extensibility, security, flexibility, and performance.

Of course, every organization in the health ecosystem is at a slightly different place in readiness and challenges. Many life sciences organizations have had fairly large clinical/biostatistical computing departments in place for decades, but those groups have been mired in a highly regulated culture, and rarely (if ever) transcend to address the commercial concerns of the organization where analytical capacity is much scarcer. Health plans have invested in modest analytical centers often focused on actuarial analysis and fraud, but these organizations often lack the scale and perspective on true clinical analytics. Health providers (especially nonacademic institutions) often lack analytical competencies beyond basic report generation; it remains to be seen whether "starting from little" is better or worse than "starting from a lot."

Wherever your organization is at today, take heart that everyone in the ecosystem faces real challenges in growing their competencies in health analytics. No one is a poster child for what it should look like. The operating models that have been effective in department-level analytics are not scalable to the enterprise. Existing centers that focus on reporting are not dealing with the real issues associated with prospective organizational decision making. In short, health analytics are an enterprise-class game—treating it as anything but an enterprise-level issue limits the applicability, reduces the effectiveness, limits the return on investment, and precludes achieving a meaningful patient-centered business transformation.

CHAPTER 4

Dealing with Data

CALLIMACHUS

The healing temples (asclepeions) in Alexandria, Kos, and other geographic centers served as the equivalent of our medical facilities today. Practitioners were located at the temple, and patients spent the night while receiving a wide variety of treatments. Despite the creative use of soporific anesthesias and crude surgical techniques, many treatments were likely of questionable value. But the temples served as a special place—a location where alleviating human suffering was the very specific goal. And before we pass judgment on our ancient brethren too quickly, one of these asclepeions still houses the medical histories of around 70 patients carved in stone—a model of information persistence we have lacked until recently.

Around 245 BCE, a poet and scholar named Callimachus worked at Alexandria's library. A passionate advocate for shorter-form writing, Callimachus was an accomplished writer and poet over the course of his life. But he spent his days sorting through thousands of literary works spread across Alexandria's huge library. If anyone ever had a data problem, it was Callimachus.

So Callimachus wrote something out of character for a short-form literature advocate: a 120-volume literary work called *The Pinakes*. This work dealt with his big data problem: it cataloged and categorized all of the authors and works of literature housed in the library. For the first time, a visitor to the library could check a source to see if an author or specific literary work was within the library, and if so, where the work might be located. *The Pinakes* was the beginning of information and library sciences as we know it today, and variations on Callimachus's methods would be used around the world for the next 2,000 years (until the advent of the Dewey Decimal system in 1876).

NOT A DROP TO DRINK

Medical records. Claims. Clinical trials. Social media. Scientific publications. Consumer purchasing. Genomics. Billing. It has taken longer than it should but health care is getting wired—physicians and hospitals have reached the tipping point in the adoption of electronic health records (EHR), data is flowing within and between institutions, and practically every medical device is a digital device.

In the classic literary work *The Rime of the Ancient Mariner*, the poet Samuel Taylor Coleridge describes the ironic situation of being adrift in a massive ocean of salt water without being able to quench a basic thirst:

> Water, water, everywhere,
> Nor any drop to drink.

In health today, we do not lack data: we lack insight from the data. But we are swimming in an ocean of data. As a matter of fact, there is so much data available to us today that it is hard to conceptualize even a small corner of the ocean of available data sources, types, and use cases. In the face of being able to drink very little of it, never before has mankind seen the opportunity to improve the human condition as it exists today. A world of knowable insights—insights actually attainable from data we already have—challenges us to step up and become smarter about the way we practice the art, science, and business of medicine.

DEFINING DATA

How much health-relevant data actually exists? Before we can answer that, let's define what we mean by health-relevant data (HRD).

Much of the industry today conceptualizes health data fairly narrowly. The term is often construed broadly to cover clinical and claims data. Health data can be perceived as data covered under privacy and security regulations such as The Health Insurance Portability and

Accountability Act (HIPAA) of 1996. The term is also used to describe population-level data such as public health data. And increasingly, simply through association, the term health data is associated with the explosive growth of electronic medical record (EMR) data.

All of those characterizations for health data are fine. But for the purposes of this book, our definition is considerably broader. Accordingly, we have adopted the term HRD. We define HRD as any data that can help an organization better understand costs, outcomes, and associated individual preferences and behaviors.

Why are we looking at data so broadly? Recall that our proposed framework for health analytics consists of a multipronged strategy of improving health outcomes, financial performance, and customer insights. So our palette of HRD is by necessity going to be broad. More importantly, since our long-term goal is linking those dimensions together, we need to start with a plan that incorporates the broadest set of available data sources and types. If any data whatsoever—regardless of source or type—can be used to better understand and influence outcomes and costs, we consider it relevant.

We characterize HRD across four broad data categories:

1. **Clinical**—data about a patient's medical observations
2. **Administrative/Operational**—data about the business processes within the health ecosystem (e.g., delivering care, research operations)
3. **Financial**—data about revenues and costs
4. **Behavioral**—data relating to the way people live their lives

As you can see, these categories map fairly closely to our multipronged approach to health analytics. Table 4.1 provides a few examples of data within each category (though it is obviously not exhaustive). As you can see, some data such as claims data can reasonably reside in more than one category.

BIG DATA

So returning to our earlier question, how much HRD actually exists today? The short answer is no one really knows because it is very difficult to measure. But here are some things that we do know:

Table 4.1 Health-Related Data Categories and Examples

Data Category	Examples of Data
Clinical	■ Clinical trials data ■ EMRs ■ Genetic and genomic profiles ■ Lab results
Administrative/Operational	■ Claims data ■ Project/process management ■ Practice management data ■ Quality and safety data
Financial	■ Claims data ■ Activity-based costing ■ Billing ■ Facility utilization and profitability
Behavioral	■ Consumer purchasing ■ Dietary data ■ Exercise data ■ Health care consumption patterns ■ Internet use data, including social media and mobile applications

■ Prior to very recent history, the overwhelming proportion of patient medical records were paper documents that could not be readily used for any sort of analyses. So over the past five years, the rate of growth of this type of data has been nothing short of phenomenal.

■ The most pervasively electronic HRD has historically been administrative data (e.g., billing, claims, registration), not clinical data. Electronic claims processing, billing, and regulatory actions such as HIPAA drove organizations to implement electronic solutions for these business processes earlier than clinical and other aspects of the business. Since administrative data invariably includes assumptions that do not reflect clinical interests (e.g., claims data is a great representation of what medical services are reimbursed, but a poor representation of the actual clinical conditions that led to the care), it has been difficult to use this information for deriving meaningful clinical insights.

- The broadest collection of electronic patient information was collected in the course of highly expensive clinical research projects, not patient care, using forms that recorded highly constrained views of a patient's health considered suitable only for the particular research project for which it was collected. And once collected and analyzed for that study, all of the data were generally shelved, rarely if ever used again.

- One of the best longitudinal clinical data sources (data tracking a given person's medical states over extended periods of time) in the United States is generally considered to be government and military health records such as those in the Veteran's Administration (VA). Though many people in the U.S. general population change care providers over time, military veterans often receive health services from the U.S. government for most of their lives. As a very early adopter of systems such as EMRs, the VA and other government organizations today have vast repositories of patient information.

So looking at our data heritage, we have some limitations. But those limitations are rapidly being overcome by the onslaught of electronic data. Each of the major market segments—providers, payers, and life sciences firms of all types—is aggressively investing in a wide array of information technology generating and collecting all four of our data types. Patients are also participating in this data explosion: personal health records, online patient communities, medical devices and monitoring, mobile health applications . . . the list grows longer every day. And, perhaps most interesting of all, there is a growing recognition that consumer and other data not traditionally associated with health care have a role to play in helping progress a more effective health care ecosystem.

Unfortunately, like other industries, health industry executives are also bombarded with marketing messages about the opportunity in big data. The analyst group Gartner projected 2013 spending on big data to top U.S. $34 billion. But before rushing into stockpiling petabytes of data, leaders should keep a few things in mind:

- If you don't know what you are going to do with data, there is no way you will collect it properly.

- "More" and "Better" are two different and often unrelated concepts.

- "More" increases costs regardless of how it is used (i.e., storage, cleaning, administration, integration architectures, licenses, etc.).

- "Better," when used properly, increases return on investment (i.e., increased efficacy, productivity, cost containment and avoidance, revenue maximization)

- If the "more" is not already inherently "better," it can only become "better" by incurring additional costs.

In summary, "more" is a quantitative assessment—one petabyte is more than 500 terabytes. "Better" is a qualitative assessment—it requires context in order to assess. In the world of analytics, that context is directly related to the questions you are trying to answer. Without that context, "more" can only ever be "more."

GROWTH IN DATA PROVISIONING

For leaders that embrace the concept of leveraging HRD, there is good news: options abound. Historically, health data licensing was a niche industry—organizations that knew how to find the precious few sources of electronic data licensed it from the data source providers, technically prepared the data, and constructed commercial products and services around the data. For example, pharmaceutical sales planning has been based on market analyses from aggregated prescription and claims information. It was a difficult but lucrative business with high barriers to entry. And since most of the data was administrative, the data was more appropriate for commercial applications as opposed to clinical or research endeavors.

But as the diversity of health-related information technologies has grown, so has an entire market dedicated to aggregating, cleaning, enhancing, and licensing data. As our appetite for data beyond administrative information grows, the market has responded.

Most of the HRD available today comes from one of six sources:

1. **Self-Generated.** When they stop and look, many organizations are surprised by how much electronic HRD they already have. Do you collect Web site traffic and visitor data? Call center records? Do you bill electronically? Do you have email/instant messaging? These systems and countless others contain HRD. As organizations undertake the creative work of identifying their critical business challenges, the need for additional data is a given. But work can usually get started with data assets already in-house.

2. **Traditional Data Vendors.** Most of the long-standing health data providers in the United States still exist today. Some of these firms have merged or been acquired by other companies that serve to diversify their commercial portfolios as the proliferation of data creates many purchasing alternatives for their customers. And in many cases, these firms have evolved to become consulting and service providers as opposed to simply data brokers.

3. **Technology Vendors.** EMR vendors, data integration middleware providers, social media, medical devices, health information exchanges, software-as-a-service (SAAS) providers . . . the list goes on. The rapid propagation of health information technologies has created an ecosystem of technology-enabled companies with their own data. Though sometimes lacking in scale, these firms nevertheless often have data sources and types that are at least novel if not proprietary.

4. **Consumer Data Providers.** Historically, consumer data aggregators—with a set of assets and services widely used by other industries—have struggled to gain traction in health and life sciences. In the past, these firms' data were most often used for marketing activities. But as our definitions of health innovation and profitability become more contingent on the unique attributes of individual patients/consumers, these firms now have new value to contribute.

5. **Consulting Aggregators.** The major global consulting and system integrators have taken on the challenges associated

with building data businesses. These businesses enable the firms to compete more effectively against other consulting firms, and the enhancements they make to the data can command a premium. Increasingly, these organizations are generating the data as well through business process outsourcing and infrastructure agreements. The combination of reusable data assets, human resource capacity, and access to analytical skill sets make these firms attractive to the larger health ecosystem players. Note that large global service organizations that traditionally have not catered to health providers and payers—contract research organizations (CROS), for example—are growing new business lines to leverage their global scale, talent pools, and data assets in this burgeoning market space.

6. **Peer plays.** One of the most interesting dynamics emerging now is the recognition that health organizations can get many of their data needs met through partnerships, not fee-based data licensing and service contracts. Recognizing their strength in numbers and the dramatically lower cost structure associated with sharing, many firms are seeing the value in shared data and expertise, especially when the partnering is around a specific problem space such as diabetes. Partnering represents a great opportunity; getting out of the darkened stadium by definition is a group effort (see Chapter 2).

So whether your organization already has the data it needs or not, there is no shortage of opportunity, and no excuses for not moving forward. So why don't more organizations already take more advantage of data?

THE EXCUSES EVERY LEADER NEEDS TO KNOW

No health leader seeking to influence transformation can expect to get very far without encountering two massive forces of resistance:

1. **Inertia (or the lack thereof).** Change is always a culturally mediated phenomenon. Whether an organization has a tradition of operating certain ways, or perhaps has a tradition of NOT

operating in certain ways, industry leaders must not under-
estimate Newton's first law of motion: objects in a certain state
of motion tend to stay in that state of motion until acted on by
another force.

2. **Fear.** Individuals differ in both their assessment and tolerance of
risk. In the face of ambiguity and uncertainty on what the future
holds, many well-motivated and talented people will nonetheless resist the forces of change.

With these two barriers as a backdrop, we offer up a few of the most
common reasons cited for avoiding progress in analytics alongside some
suggestions for how leaders should conceptualize the objections. As is
always the case, a healthy dose of empathy (with a booster of leadership) never hurts as well.

"We don't have enough electronic data."

Given the big data discussions so common across enterprises today,
it is surprising how often this excuse still surfaces. No organization ever
has enough of four assets: money, people, time, and data. But every
organization has some of all of them. The measure of enough data can
only be answered analytically—it is not a reason to stop progress;
rather, it is one of the first questions that should be asked analytically.
And just like people, money, and time, what you do with however
much you have makes all the difference.

"The data we have isn't good enough."

If the first analytical excuse is data volume, the second is usually
data suitability (and these excuses are usually given at the same time).
And like the first excuse, it is a reason to move forward, not hold back.
Shortcomings in volume and suitability become continuous improvement initiatives for the enterprise, but they never get surfaced if
enterprise-class advanced analytical initiatives never get off the ground.
We need to be able to quantify "good enough."

"We need more standards before our data is usable."

In the health IT world, there is a common saying: the great thing
about standards is everybody has their own. There are three stark
realities that leaders need to understand about standards. First, there
are ample standards today, but organizations fail to use them consistently. Second, standards come into force not from committees and

industry bodies—their power comes only from real-world use. And third, real-world use should include the needs of health analytics. So if a lack of standards plagues your information management competencies (and it undoubtedly does), health analytics is your opportunity to let the intended use of the data drive the upstream process of standardizing the data.

"We can't use the data because it is not integrated. We need a new data warehouse."

Health care, like many other industries, is littered with the past failures of data warehousing initiatives. Consultants, technology vendors, and well-meaning people have sought to simplify the complexities of information-based decision making through the lets-get-all-the-data-in-one-bucket project. With historical project failure rates hitting as high as two out of three, every executive should be skeptical of both the value and the feasibility of data warehouse projects as cure-alls for health insights.

Industry leaders need to know three things.

1. A data's physical location is not usually on the critical path of deriving insights from it; compared to the myriad of other issues we're talking about in this book, "where" is one of the lesser concerns.

2. Data structures within data warehouses actually run counter to most analytical needs. When an analytical project gets underway, one of the first things that happens is data gets restructured into something more suitable for analysis.

3. Modern analytical software doesn't really care where data is stored—it expects to combine data from all over the place. So if you have a data warehouse, that's great. But if you don't, that's not a problem either . . . the software can go to wherever the data is located, and it is going to restructure it anyway.

"We can't get access to the data—the technology is poor."

This excuse is common in dealing with proprietary or otherwise closed sources of data, including many EMR systems. With today's software, there are virtually no limitations to data access that cannot be overcome with a little time, creativity, and occasional brute force. Even in the worst situations, techniques such as reverse-engineering data models, direct access to physical storage, and even screen scraping (an ugly but sometimes necessary computerized technique for copying data directly from a computer's monitor) are used to overcome the technical shortcomings associated with outdated, poorly architected, or otherwise inflexible system designs. And almost always, the solutions are more timely and elegant than those extreme cases.

"We can't get access to the data—the regulations prevent it."

There is no question that regulations place constraints (rightly so) on our ability to collect, aggregate, and use health-related information. In some cases, these challenges are real and appropriate. In others, the barriers represent over-generalizations, misunderstanding of policy/regulatory concerns, or in many cases myths of how an organization must operate.

All health leaders must give careful consideration and high priority to data privacy, security, and compliance concerns. But they also need to make sure employees are educated about real versus perceived constraints. And they need to make sure that policies and procedures protect the concerns of patients and the regulatory risks to the organization while at the same time creating opportunities for innovations and improvements. Both patients and regulators have a shared desire to improve health outcomes and lower costs, and they are both looking to institutions to do the right thing.

"You can't draw meaningful conclusions from statistics."

We base medical decisions, policies, and practices on data and analytics every hour of the day. Every prescription drug approved and dispensed in the United States for over 20 years was assessed for both safety and efficacy using statistics. This excuse is sometimes an indicator of fear—individuals believing that their contributions in an organization (role, prestige, demand, potentially even compensation) will somehow be diminished if computers become involved in business operations. The excuse is also sometimes an indication that more education is needed on what analytics are all about, and how they are used alongside people-based assets such as education, experience, instinct and judgment. In short, we don't expect analytical software to be the decision maker—we expect it to support decision makers in new and more powerful ways.

BUILDING FOR TOMORROW

Having given you a list of commonly cited excuses, it is also important to highlight that there are significant challenges in data as well. It is not all roses, and it is definitely not easy.

Data Pedigree

In a world where data is pouring over our organizational embankments, one of the real challenges is knowing—over time—the history of a given piece of data. Where did it come from? Under what conditions and constraints was it collected? What if anything has happened to it since this copy of the data was created? Though these may seem like academic questions, they become very real in some cases. For example, was this data subsequently found to be fraudulent? Was there an error in data collection that someone eventually found and corrected? Has a human being ever even looked at this data before, or has it always lived outside the visibility of human scrutiny? How trustworthy is the data source? Our data disciplines will eventually need to confront these issues if we are to continue to improve the value of our information assets.

Data Context

It is also important that we strive to understand the medical context under which data was collected in the first place, which is similar but distinct from understanding the history of a data item. For example, a patient's medical record may indicate that her pulse on a certain date was 78. But what does that value mean? Was the patient in a resting state, or did she just finish a treadmill exercise? Was the patient taking any medications at the time that may be influencing her cardiovascular rate? Was the measurement taken in the course of a normal annual physical exam, or during a heart attack? In short, it is just as important to know the conditions surrounding a data item as it is to know the measurement itself.

Master Data Management

For two decades, health organizations have sought to develop and implement master patient indices—common patient identifiers that allow organizations to link disparate information about the same patient together. Mary might be called Patient #394856 in an EMR system, Patient #6A209 in the scheduling system, and #Mary7635 on the self-service portal. How can we get a single view of Mary across the enterprise?

With the adoption of health information exchanges alongside the burgeoning use of third-party data sources, the needs for uniquely identifying a single human (under the right privacy constraints) is rising. Master data management, as this competency is termed in other industries, has a growing role to play in health care, though it remains to be seen how widely, quickly, and effectively existing techniques can be married to the unique privacy and regulatory concerns inherent in health care. Solutions exist today, but this space is also under construction.

Resource Allocation

Every institution struggles with resource capacity. There just never seems to be enough people to do all of the things that need doing. And unfortunately, health analytics can exacerbate this problem. Industry leaders face tough tradeoff decisions when determining whether to staff new analytical initiatives. Though additional capacity can be secured (at a cost) through contracted resources, there is no avoiding an inevitable hit on internal staff, and so leaders and managers are well advised to:

a) Contain scope.

b) Clearly communicate expectations.

c) Carefully monitor the business value derived from these initiatives.

Skill Coverage

It is a big question: will health organizations (especially providers) staff analytical expertise? The consulting firms are betting that their customers will choose not to build analytical competencies in-house, thereby ensuring an ongoing revenue stream for consultants. In many cases, consulting talent is probably a great option. But our position is that, regardless of the total capacity that you choose to insource versus outsource, health firms of all types need some level of analytical talent in-house. Why? Because analytics are required to be competitive, and you cannot fully outsource your company's competitiveness. That does not mean that you need to hire 100 statisticians; it just means you need at least two analytics experts that can serve to guide your company's evolution towards richer data-driven decisions.

Information Management

Chapter 3 covered a number of challenges in taking on health analytics that are worth repeating here:

- **Time.** Introducing time as an analytical dimension is a necessary but sometimes challenging aspect of working with data.

- **Validity and Reliability.** We said earlier that the objection *"the data we have isn't good enough"* is an excuse. But it can also be real. You can tell the difference between the excuse and the real issue by whether anyone has statistically investigated the validity and reliability of the data.

- **Data Quality.** Though extremely rare exceptions might exist, as a general rule, no company's data is as clean as they think, and no company's data is ready for proper analysis.

- **Data Governance.** It is very hard to develop enterprise-level processes, shared asset creation, and decisions, especially when dealing with something as potentially complicated as data. Health organizations need to be able to institutionalize the processes associated with establishing and managing "core" data assets; the identification, acquisition, and onboarding of new data sources; and the strategic decision making on analytical priorities.

Note that the master data management challenge we just discussed is a specific case of information management challenges (data governance and quality).

CONCLUSION

Despite these challenges, our industry is moving forward in new and exciting ways. Our very understanding of HRD is changing rapidly over time. As new perspectives on prognostic forces that influence health outcomes emerge, and as new sources of electronic data become available, we see an ever-increasing landscape of data from which to derive insights.

We need to dismantle the assumption that health organizations will develop a fixed portfolio of data assets from which their businesses will be optimized. The questions are infinite. The sources of data are infinite. The volume of data is infinite. The challenge that health leaders face is not how to create a data library; rather, the question is how to create a responsive information competency within their enterprise.

Said another way, if:

- Your market is changing,
- Your needs are changing,
- The opportunities for insights are ever-growing,

then trying to "standardize" your business could be a recipe for competitive disadvantage and a fast track to obsolescence. It's not that you don't want to optimize—of course you do; efficiency drives profitability. But the goal should be to optimize: a) your ability to derive insights, and b) your responsiveness to those insights. These are how health analytics guide transformation.

Getting Off the Bench

CASE STUDY

Is it really possible to develop a common set of data and analytical assets that can be leveraged for multiple purposes? Even through a self-service environment for nontechnical staff? One Southeast hospital has done just that.

The 795-bed organization developed a strategy for combining internal hospital data with external data sources in order to offer staff direct insights into a wide variety of enterprise issues, including:

- Care benchmarks
- Nursing workloads and staffing models
- Health services research
- Patient risk scoring
- Adverse-event detection and patient safety indicators
- Patient survey results
- Lab-processing efficiency

(continued)

- Rural health-threat assessment and prevention
- Assessing and improving the quality of third-party data

In addition, the comparison benchmarks and metrics generated are considered by staff to be more reliable and compelling because advanced analytics normalize the benchmarking process against the unique attributes of the hospital and its patients.

CHAPTER **5**

BEST Care, First Time, Every Time

By Dr. Graham Hughes

Chief Medical Officer, SAS Center for Health Analytics and Insights

Many pivotal moments in our personal and professional lives have appeared utterly trivial at the time, only to resurface years or even decades later. A seed of an idea is planted and then filed away, lying dormant until a seemingly random event unlocks the idea, and it begins to grow towards its full significance.

It has been a combination of these small yet significant events that have influenced my thinking about the nature of clinical outcomes and the ways in which a health care system can systematically improve those outcomes.

MEDICINE: ART, SCIENCE, OR BOTH?

It was as a medical student, and later as a junior doctor, at Kings College Hospital in London, that one of these seeds was first planted by Professor Michael Baum. Over the duration of his internationally renowned career as a surgical oncologist specializing in breast cancer treatment, Professor Baum has at times been a somewhat controversial figure. This is at least in part due to his aggressive stance on the critical importance of the scientific method as a foundation for understanding comparative effectiveness of treatment options. He was among the first medical researchers to provide clear evidence, through randomized controlled clinical trials, of the value of adjuvant oral chemotherapy in early stage breast cancer. His research led to a dramatic reduction in the level of disfiguring surgery to women with breast cancer, while concurrently contributing to a 30% reduction in disease-related mortality.

The corollary of Professor Baum's evangelism of the importance of data-driven health care has been his criticism of unevaluated alternative medicine. He has described homeopathy as a cruel deception, essentially equivalent to the use of bloodletting and purgatives as cure-alls in the 19th century. In an open letter to Prince Charles, Baum rebuked the prince for his stance on alternative medicine, writing "the power of my authority comes with a knowledge based on 40 years of study and 25 years of active involvement in cancer research. . . . Your power and authority rest on an accident of birth." As you might now imagine, any conversation you have with Dr. Baum has the potential to be memorable.

His approach was, and is, perfectly in keeping with one of the key tenants of medical ethics: First, Do No Harm. Dr. Baum lets the data inform the decision. Where insufficient data exists to guide a decision, he works tirelessly to build sufficient evidence to support or disprove the value of a medical intervention.

One day, Dr. Baum asked a small group of medical students who had collected in his office a question, "If you were each to draw a line with 'art' and 'science' representing polar opposite ends of that line, where would you place a point that effectively describes the practice of medicine?" (See Figure 5.1) Though his question felt like a somewhat contrived parlor game at the time, it has influenced my thinking of evidence-based medicine to this day. Baum's challenge was simply to provoke us to think more deeply about the quality of scientific evidence that supported much of the training that we had received and would be using as the foundation of day-to-day interactions with patients. How much of what we had learned was unshakeable truth?

Figure 5.1 The Traditional Art Versus Science Conundrum.

How much was anecdotal or dogmatic? How much of our decision making would require going beyond the boundaries of what was a clear cut decision?

Today, Baum's challenge feels more important than ever. For every patient that we manage and for every condition that we propose a series of interventions, to what extent are those decisions made on a strong foundation of scientific evidence, and to what extent does that evidence apply to the management of this specific individual? If both caregivers and patients ask these questions, we stand a much better chance of going no further than the current best evidence supports. And when we choose to go beyond that evidence, we do it with clear consideration of the additional risks that may be placed on the patient.

When we think about the age-old question of Medicine as Art versus Medicine as Science, we need to reframe Professor Baum's overly constrained single-axis model in favor of a two-axis model where patient-specific care decisions must be weighed against: a) the current level of medical evidence, and b) the level to which unique judgment must be applied to address the specific needs of the individual (see Figure 5.2). In this way we can recognize what is already widely understood by most health care professionals: every patient encounter requires a unique application of both art and science.

One might argue that with increasing levels of scientific evidence, the art of medicine becomes less and less important. In essence, the preponderance of evidence of best practices can become so overwhelming that a robot could do just as good a job at recommending the most appropriate course of therapy. In the most trivial of circumstances, this may be possible, but treatment plans will always need to be tweaked and refined to meet the needs of the individual patient.

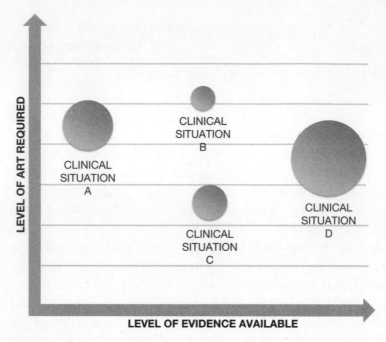

Figure 5.2 Patient-Centric "Art and Science" Model.

LEVERAGING EVIDENCE TO DELIVER IMPROVED OUTCOMES

Good medicine is not just about knowing what the current evidence shows; it is also about being able to apply that knowledge to the unique circumstances presented by each individual patient.

When it comes to articulating this delicate balance between standardization and individualization of treatment, few do so as eloquently and frequently as Dr. Brent James of Intermountain Healthcare. Dr. James is a strong proponent for the broad adoption of rigorous quality systems rooted in W. Edwards Deming's principles, and with a Toyota-like focus on optimizing frontline work. He not only successfully advocates for application of those principles to frontline care at Intermountain Healthcare, but also regularly delivers that same message to health care leaders from around the world in a four-month course called the Advanced Training Program (ATP). James argues that, although we have made great strides over the past century or so, the medical profession is still susceptible to practicing the craft of medicine in which personal experience takes on a greater role than it should, and frequently leads to practices based on "my professional opinion" rather than "according to the broadly available evidence."

I have had the pleasure of attending an accelerated version of Dr. James' ATP class, and it was during that course that additional seeds took root in my mind. Dr. James provides countless examples of the ways in which careful analysis of existing patterns of care, combined with a clinically led approach to care quality improvement, have led to sustained transformations that consistently deliver higher quality care and improved outcomes. He lets the data do the talking, seeking to understand the root causes of variation and the impact of those variations on clinical outcomes rather than to eliminate variations altogether.

That's the first seed. Recognize that some variations in care are appropriate and some are not. In other words, always assume that care providers are trying to deliver the best possible care, and work closely with them to identify which patterns of care delivery work most effectively and which do not. This helps to alleviate one of the most frequent concerns that physicians have when they feel that they are being measured—that the best practice "cookbook" doesn't take into account the nuances of their patient populations. Keep an open mind, let the data do the talking and seek to collaborate to improve care at both the individual and population level rather than dictating a one-size-fits-all best practice.

Dr. James is a strong advocate of applying care guidelines to eliminate inappropriate variation, but his mantra that "no individual guideline applies completely to any individual patient" has helped to create a culture of learning at Intermountain Healthcare with a data-driven focus on improving outcomes. Everyone has the opportunity to contribute to development and adoption of clinical best practices, and everyone has the opportunity to advance the understanding of when variation from a guideline makes sense and when it doesn't. Intermountain Healthcare manages what it measures, and it measures an ever-increasing proportion of care delivery provided across its health-care delivery system.

The second seed relates to the ways in which knowledge is disseminated and consumed. Dr. James explains that there is strong experimental evidence that human beings (and yes that includes doctors) are demonstrably only capable of processing up to seven variables at any one time. This information, which supports Dr. David Eddy's frequently cited assertion that the increasing level of complexity in health care exceeds the unaided capacity of the human mind, made me think differently about how medical practice should evolve in a world with ever-increasing levels of technology and digitization. Why, in this new era of rapidly evolving medical knowledge combined with ever increasing medical technology innovation, are most electronic medical record (EMR) systems still being designed to replicate paper charts designed for a prior era? Instead we need to take the opportunity to build software applications that are capable of analyzing increasingly large patient data sets to both derive best practices from existing data and to provide decision support tools to help improve clinical decision making. If car drivers can take advantage of digital mapping products and GPS systems to help them find the most efficient route to their destination, why can't medicine?

WHAT ARE CLINICAL OUTCOMES?

Clinical outcomes are the results of health care interventions.

Of course, that's a very general statement begging for further clarification. For example, do outcomes represent the short- or long-term results of an individual intervention? Are outcomes patient-centric or population-centric? Do outcomes primarily represent the perspective of the physician or the patient and perhaps other stakeholders, such as health plans, employers, and the government? What defines a health care intervention?

Here's where another seed was planted. A number of years ago, I remember listening to Dr. Denis Cortese, who at that time was the CEO of the world-famous Mayo Clinic, in his chairman's remarks during a workshop on evidence-based medicine. He drew an interesting analogy between value in health care and the value of a pair of shoes. Dr. Cortese said that he was wearing a pair of three-month-old shoes that he really liked. He said that at that moment in time, it appeared to him that they were excellent value. But if those shoes fell apart within the next six months, his perception of the value of those shoes would change dramatically. Just as we can only understand the value of a pair of shoes as a function of expectation and utility over time, the same applies to health care value. We need to understand the results of health care interventions over time to truly assess clinical outcomes.

One relatively unequivocal and frequently used outcome measure is mortality. Not much room for disagreement on that measure—you're either dead or you're not. However, before that measure is reached, there are a variety of significant condition- and intervention-specific measures that change over time:

- **Physiological Values**—for example, blood pressure, peak flow levels, lab values, etc.
- **Clinical Events**—stroke, post-operative infection rates, and readmissions
- **Symptoms**—pain, difficulty breathing, anxiety
- **Functional Measures**—the SF-36 health survey, ability to walk up a flight of stairs, ability to read in low light, etc.
- **Patient Experience Measures**—patient satisfaction surveys, level of understanding of the plan of care, etc.

When weighing the most appropriate course of action for an individual patient, there are a number of factors that must be considered including, and perhaps most importantly, the level of evidence to indicate that the benefits of the intervention exceed the risks (see Figure 5.3). This may sound obvious, but there are many occasions when patients are subjected to health care interventions where the benefit is uncertain and the level of risk is significant. For example, for many years it was believed that aggressive therapy for breast cancer (such as radical mastectomy) must improve survival rates for breast cancer. We now have strong evidence that disproves that theory, but many women were subjected to unnecessary and disfiguring surgery even though there was no evidence that the benefit outweighed the risks. Similarly, there are more recent examples where patients without significant heart disease have undergone cardiac catheterization, angioplasty, and stenting even though the actual benefit is unclear or absent.

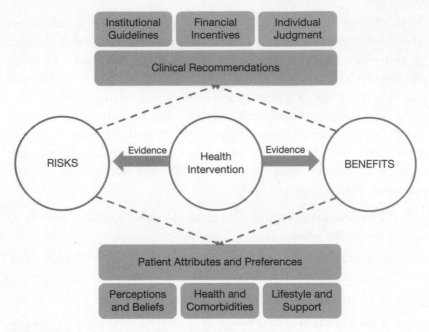

Figure 5.3 Intervention and Outcome Considerations.

Some of the additional factors that need to be considered when recommending a course of action for an individual patient are shown in Figure 5.3. Let's take a closer look at the elements of this diagram:

- **Health Care Intervention.** A health care intervention can represent any treatment or therapy option considered for the patient. Health care interventions include short- or long-term medication therapy, admission to hospital, surgical procedures, application or administration of medical devices, and other therapeutic options, including diets and lifestyle recommendations.

- **Evidence.** This represents the levels to which evidence is available that quantifies the anticipated benefits as well as the risks associated with a particular health care intervention. The U.S. Preventative Services Taskforce (USPSTF) stratifies the quality of the available evidence on a scale from 1 to 3, where 1 is the best available evidence (derived from at least one well conducted randomized clinical trial) and 3 represents opinions of respected authorities and descriptions of clinical experience.

- **Benefits.** Benefits represent the positive clinical outcomes that can reasonably be expected at any point in time after this specific health care intervention, based on the current evidence. It does not factor in the financial benefit associated with lower cost interventions. The outcomes may be measured and described in one or more of the outcomes categories indicated in the figure. For example, the long term survival of a particular hip replacement may not be as long as another, but if the speed of return to full function is faster and the complication rates are lower, then the risk/benefit balance of outcomes may tip in favor of the shorter-lasting hip.

- **Risks.** Risks are the undesirable clinical outcomes that have been observed as associated with the health care intervention. Risks are usually quantified by their frequency of occurrence as well as the severity of the negative outcome.

- **Clinical Recommendations.** The clinician weighs the available evidence to provide one or more recommended treatment options for the patient to consider. Each recommendation will typically have its unique levels of evidence as well as a unique profile of risk/benefit. Although clinicians try to remain as objective as possible and to recommend the treatment option that is both the most advantageous and suitable for the patient, there are external pressures that may influence their recommendation to a greater or lesser extent. Some of those pressures include financial incentives and disincentives (such as fee-for-service payment and institutional reward models), institutional guidelines (such as approved formularies or other standards), and individual experience and preference.

- **Patient Attributes and Preferences.** These are the factors that make each individual unique. They range from patient health status, age, including severity of illness and comorbidities, prior therapy, patient lifestyle, motivation, income level, insurance coverage, support structure, access to primary care as well as other personal, cultural, and religious beliefs. The patient's goals as well as his or her assessment of risk/benefit need to be considered carefully with the goal of achieving shared decision making.

Given all of the preceding, it is not hard to see why Chapter 1 of this book proposes that "complexity exceeds cognition."

SUPPLEMENTING THE UNAIDED HUMAN MIND

In one of the most quoted papers on psychology ever written, George Armitage Miller claimed that he had been persecuted by an integer. That integer was the number 7. Over a period of seven years, his research had shown that human beings were capable of processing seven (plus or minus two) variables at any one time. In fact, more recent research has shown that the number might actually be closer to four, rather than seven.

Most of us experience this challenge every day. In this increasingly wired and information intense world, we are interrupted every three to five minutes during the course of a work day, multitasking between email notifications, text messages, cellphone calls, chat requests, and reviewing Web sites. We frequently end up getting distracted and temporarily forget what we were working on moments ago. Our cultures are increasingly tailored to information junkies, and digital connectivity has radically increased the flow of data to feed the habit—yet our cognitive capacity is reasonably fixed.

Physicians and other caregivers are pattern matchers by training. They rely on their extensive knowledge base, built painstakingly over many years of training, practice, and ongoing education, to identify key signals in a patient's presentation that will point to the most likely diagnosis, treatment options, and ongoing day-to-day management. Sometimes it doesn't take seven variables to safely determine the most appropriate next steps in weighing evaluation and treatment options. But going forward, delivering the *best* care, first time, every time, will require looking at many more variables. As an industry, and as medical practitioners, we are obligated to use the best information possible in making decisions, but the challenge in doing that is growing exponentially.

The doubling time of medical knowledge is currently estimated to be less than ten years, and that time span is decreasing rapidly. The volume of medical literature that a busy doctor needs to read to stay current keeps increasing, and all too frequently different research reports present apparently contradictory evidence. Frequently, no single treatment approach is suitable for all cases. And as in all other aspects of our lives, the amount of useful, interpretable health data being collected is growing at an explosive rate (see Figure 5.4).

When you consider these data growth factors, combined with the pressure to maintain quality while seeing increasing volumes of patients, it's easy to understand why many doctors today feel that there has to be a different and more satisfying way to deliver the high quality care that they believe is possible. They are eager to jump off the current "hamster wheel" of medicine.

The truth is that doctors, like all humans, are excellent pattern matchers but highly fallible complex information processors. They are also not "perfectible"—we all make occasional mistakes, some more serious than others. We tend to overly simplify complex issues and our recent personal experience weighs more heavily than it should when good evidence exists to the contrary. The bottom line is that health care has to change to accommodate these dynamics.

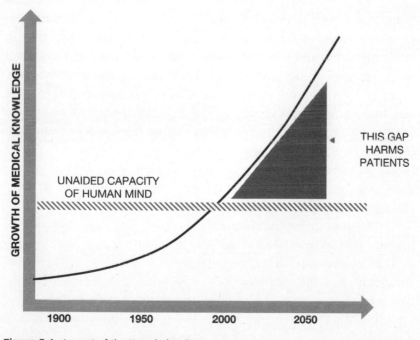

Figure 5.4 Impact of the Knowledge Gap.

HEALTH CARE'S DARK FIBER

As discussed in Chapter 4, we already have more health care data than we know what to do with. It is currently stored in large, often disparate silos and in a highly fragmented state. Demographic data, admission and appointment data, claims data, clinical trials data, laboratory data, medication prescription and administration data, interventional and noninterventional diagnostic data, as well as medical and nursing notes, and assessments. There are clearly huge amounts of medical data available today and the vast majority of those data remain unanalyzed or dramatically under-analyzed.

It's not really surprising; the systems that generate those data were seldom purchased with future analysis in mind, and the pressure to respond to organizational imperatives with additional automation tends to overwhelm even the most forward-thinking leaders. But at some stage, it comes time to consider how best to leverage the assets you have, and how to architect for the ongoing curation and analysis of the data that you will have.

In the late 1990's, during the dot-com boom, telecommunications and media companies anticipated the future demand for extremely high bandwidth communications channels locally, regionally, nationally, and internationally. They were quick to envisage a future where on-demand digital streaming multimedia was the norm and that existing infrastructure was clearly inadequate. There was the equivalent of an arms race to create and own optic fiber bandwidth and each company started laying hundreds of thousands of miles of ultra-high capacity optic cable in anticipation of the future demand. For a long time most of that fiber was just sitting there waiting to be used at a future date. The term "dark fiber" emerged to describe this unused capacity.

And that describes health care today. "Dark data"—pools of health-relevant data at rest, hardly ever touched, and usually dormant. Big data advocates often refer to the three V's: Volume, Velocity, and Variability. And those definitely describe health information. But the win for patients, payers, and providers is the fourth V-Value. Our industry's triple aim—better health, better care, lower costs—is only achievable when we begin to unlock this dark data.

This book covers a tremendous landscape of analytical opportunity across the health ecosystem, all of which are intended to address the triple aim. As you look across these opportunities, some common themes emerge, themes that hopefully will serve as seeds for you in thinking about how to pursue data-driven innovation. Some of these themes include:

1. **Assessing and Managing Clinical and Financial Risk.** Gaining a deeper data-driven understanding of clinical and financial risk-both at the individual and population level.

2. **Focusing on Prospective Care Quality.** Expanding and supplementing existing EMR-based clinical decision support systems (CDSSs) with richer clinical signals detected using advanced analytics. The signals identify opportunities to intervene earlier and avert patient harm.

3. **Targeting Opportunities for Care Efficiency.** Improved understanding of the basis for both appropriate and inappropriate variability in both the cost and quality of care delivery.

4. **Improving Patient Outreach and Engagement.** Blending traditional health care data with other consumer and social information in order to better understand individual patients' propensities towards behaviors and actions—patient characteristics that should be informing more personalized patient engagement decisions.

5. **Managing Data and Knowledge Curation.** There are vast stores of poorly curated knowledge in all health care organizations, from the increasingly tangled web of metadata that associates meaning to the data in storage, through the patterns in clinical care delivery that are not formalized into any formalized template driven structure. Analytics can help identify complex patterns in existing data and provide significant insight to help automate the ongoing challenge of institutional knowledge management.

IDENTIFYING HIDDEN PATTERNS

I've shared several seed moments in my life that have influenced how I see medicine today. I will conclude this chapter by sharing an event that has shaped my perspectives on health information technology and systems.

The event occurred nearly 20 years ago, while rolling out one of the first ever whole-hospital EMR systems. It was a brand new 450-bed hospital in Glasgow, Scotland, and we were in the process of implementing a big software vendor's complete suite: EMR, results reporting, computerized physician order entry, and documentation. We had no plans for any paper storage at all, so obviously that implementation was a roller coaster ride.

I was walking through the Intensive Care Unit six months or so after the hospital had opened its doors. We probably had about eight patients in the unit at the time. An anesthesiologist was staring intently at the results reporting screen for a specific patient of interest, and in particular at a software feature that allowed the user to review very large sets of results. This view didn't actually show discrete result values itself; rather, it showed a summary view of all discrete results, color-coding an indication if a result was abnormally high (red) or low (blue). The user could then zoom in to particular areas of interest.

As I observed this anesthesiologist working, I noticed that he was zoomed all the way out. I wondered why he didn't just click on the small window to navigate to the specific result of interest, so I asked him. His answer was both curious and delightful. It stopped me in my tracks and still does whenever I think about it.

He said, "You see that pattern of blue and red . . . well, it kind of looks like a seahorse doesn't it? I've seen that kind of seahorse pattern before and I'm pretty sure that it means this patient is beginning to go into renal failure."

So a doctor who had not looked at any actual test result was reasonably confident in diagnosing incipient renal failure. He used a tool that was never intended to display "seahorses," and did what humans do best: he pattern matched, and suddenly here was an emergent property of a system that had never been anticipated or intentionally designed. I still think about what insights we might be able to gain if we intentionally designed analytical applications to create visual patterns that could be used to make synoptic sense of an ever-increasing deluge of patient data . . . tools designed specifically to reduce signal-to-noise ratio, and find the needle in the proverbial haystack of patient data.

Whether we are dealing with simple forecasting, complex predictions, or seahorses, one thing appears quite clear to me now: the art and science of medicine can converge. New combinations of data, advanced analytics, and the pattern-matching capabilities of the human mind can accomplish things that no software or single practitioner can attain. When we move beyond retrospective reporting and shift our focus to detailed, prospective, and individualized decision making, we satisfy Professor Baum's demand for evidence while also reaching for the right variations in care and costs. And every insight we produce—the seeds of future innovations in health outcomes—bring us that much closer to a world where we really can deliver the best care the first time and every time.

CHAPTER 6

Financial Performance and Reimbursement

GOALS

In health care, it is almost impossible to separate financial management and risk management. And the current movements away from fee-for-service contracts, while healthy and necessary, increase the interdependencies between revenue, cost, and risk. Whereas historically payers were the primary entity in the risk business, today all of the health ecosystem participants in one form or another are incurring and managing financial risk (including patients).

Alongside health insurance marketplaces and electronic medical records (EMRs), changes in health reimbursement have been one of the top industry debates over the past few years. And many of the discussions are not new. During earlier decades, similar issues arose with integrated delivery networks, health maintenance organizations (HMOs), and managed care. Unfortunately, many of those experiences were unsuccessful in improving quality while controlling costs.

But failures teach us how to improve. Despite the diversity, complexity, and ambiguity that currently characterize financial strategies across health and life sciences, progress is being made. We are gradually

Table 6.1 Drivers in Improving Financial Performance

Encourage	Avoid
▪ High-quality, efficient, and patient-centered care ▪ Innovations in efficiency and outcomes ▪ Tighter alignment with patient preferences ▪ Accountability for controllable quality and costs ▪ Care coordination across providers ▪ Patient participation in care decisions ▪ Patient choices that improve outcomes and costs	▪ Rewarding inefficient, ineffective, or unnecessary care ▪ Rewarding under-treatment or avoidance of at-risk patients ▪ Rewarding medical errors or adverse events ▪ Accountability for uncontrollable quality and costs ▪ Cost shifting or zero-sum economics ▪ Rewarding short-term cost reductions at the expense of long-term cost and quality issues ▪ Additional administrative cost burdens

reaching consensus on at least what the drivers should be in improving financial performance. Table 6.1 highlights some of the key desires commonly expressed in pursuing reforms, restructuring, and novel contracting models.

Even to the most ambitious and risk tolerant of industry leaders, this list is daunting. How can we hope to achieve so many goals, especially with so many interdependencies? At first glance, some of the goals may even appear somewhat contradictory: how can we encourage the inherent risk-taking in innovation and also foster stronger accountability for quality and costs? Further, the list clearly illustrates how clinical, financial, and administrative issues cannot be easily separated.

The math needed to support this list of goals will not be found in today's reports. It does not consist of retrospective, descriptive statistics of an organization's internal data. Addressing these issues requires collaboration and more sophisticated forms of analytics that focus on greater granularity around costs, causal relationships, and methods for optimization.

STRUCTURES AND MODELS

Current trends around health reimbursement and financial performance are focused on developing new models of risk-reward incentives and value-based designs. It is difficult to discuss many of these trends because the industry has yet to reach consensus on what will be useful, profitable, or otherwise successful. We sometimes struggle with even consistently defining some of the business concepts.

Most people would generally agree that the industry is moving away from purely volume-based business models. Pharmaceutical companies are being asked to bring more to the table than new drugs; they need to demonstrate stronger comparative effectiveness with existing therapies, and more effective targeting of drug therapies to individual patient characteristics. Providers are being asked to move away from transactional fee-for-service revenue models toward business models that reflect value: efficiency; quality; outcomes; and longer-term, more comprehensive relationships with patients. Payers that have managed risk and reimbursement across large populations of patients are now pursuing coverage models more tailored to individual members/patients. We use many words to describe these evolutions— consumer-driven health care, evidence-based medicine, personalized medicine, and others—but they all point to a market shifting toward greater precision in costs, outcomes, and performance.

As it relates to the reimbursement aspects of health transformation, pay-for-performance (P4P) is an umbrella concept used to describe our industry's shift from volume-based, fee-for-service compensation to other models that are more focused on the outcomes (clinical and financial) delivered. Led by many initiatives sponsored by the Centers for Medicare and Medicaid Services (CMS) and others, the industry is exploring multiple models for delivering P4P. Some of the more commonly discussed programs and initiatives are:

- **Accountable Care Organization (ACO)**—a group of providers that agrees to be accountable for the quality, cost, and overall care of a group of Medicare beneficiaries. ACOs are a legal entity focused on achieving health care quality goals and outcomes that result in cost savings.
  - **Shared Savings Program (SSP)**—an ACO program whereby physicians are financially rewarded for lowering expenses while still meeting performance standards and operating under a fee-for-service model.

- **Pioneer ACO Model**—a more ambitious ACO program designed for organizations already experienced in providing care coordination. It includes higher levels of savings and risks as compared to SSP, and enables participating organizations to transition away from fee-for-service reimbursement models. It also extends the outcomes-based payment model to payers other than Medicare.
- **Advance Payment ACO Model**—a program available to SSP participants who need additional start-up resources to build the necessary infrastructure to support the ACO. The program provides upfront and monthly payments for purposes of investment.

- **Patient-Centered Medical Home (PCMH)**—an organized community of providers focused on comprehensive, patient-centered coordinated care. PCMHs usually strive for greater accessibility by patients to care services and shared decision making. They generally seek to improve quality, safety, evidence-based practices, and prevention as a means of controlling costs. The concept of a PCMH is central to many ACOs.

- **Bundled Payments (BP)**—a method of provider reimbursement whereby payments are based on predetermined expected costs for clinically defined groupings of care services. Also known as episode-based payment, episode payment, episode-of-care payment, case rate, evidence-based case rate, global bundled payment, global payment, package pricing, and packaged pricing.

- **Value-Based Purchasing (VBP)**—a model of reimbursement whereby providers are rewarded for meeting predefined quality and efficiency performance targets. Also known as Value-Based Payments.

- **Comprehensive Care Payment (CCP)**—a model of reimbursement whereby providers are paid a single price to deliver all of the services needed for a population of patients for a fixed period of time. Also known as condition-adjusted capitation and risk-adjusted global fees.

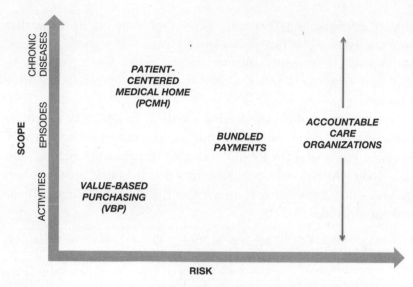

Figure 6.1 A Sample of Value-Based Models by Scope and Risk.

There are so many more structures, models, programs, initiatives, and demonstrations than these in today's rapidly evolving health ecosystem. The two features that typically characterize the main differences in these models are:

1. **Scope**—is the program attempting to address individual service costs, groups of services, and/or chronic disease management?

2. **Risk**—is the program shifting a small amount of risk to providers, is the shift more aggressive, and how is the risk shared?

Figure 6.1 illustrates how some of these concepts compare in terms of scope and risk. The list is not comprehensive, and the comparisons are not perfect, but we can use this list as a starting point for exploring how analytics can be used to drive effective changes in financial management.

MANY NAMES, COMMON ATTRIBUTES

For purposes of this discussion, we are accepting a widespread industry assumption that better quality care produces lower costs. Though that assumption has been the subject of some debate, evidence does exist to support this hypothesis, and most people generally acknowledge that since the converse is true—poor quality care undoubtedly increases health costs—it is reasonable to assume better quality results in decreased total costs (though the distribution of costs may vary considerably).

We can expect diversity in reimbursement and delivery structures and models for quite some time. But this diversity does not actually represent much of a barrier in developing our analytics strategy and plan. Many of the emerging reimbursement models share certain attributes that derive directly from the goals described above. These attributes include:

- Payments are value-based, not volume-based, focusing on evidence-driven practices and actual outcomes obtained.

- Payments cover broader or full range of services that produce good quality and outcomes, including reimbursement of services not currently covered but that can improve quality and outcomes (e.g., care coordination, education, prevention, monitoring, e-mail and phone contacts, telemedicine, etc.).

- Cost and outcome assessments that influence reimbursement and benchmarking must be sensitive to patient-specific risks and other factors.

- Variable financial obligations include both upside (i.e., rewarding good outcomes at lower costs) and downside (i.e., penalizing poor outcomes at higher costs). This includes the idea of health care warranties.

Though these attributes may at first glance appear to simply be contractual terms, there are underlying questions behind each attribute that: a) represent considerable risks for organizations that do not have the answers, and b) are questions that analytics can answer. Some of the important questions that will drive financial performance are indicated in Figure 6.2, though there are many more questions than these as well. Note also that the questions are interrelated; for example, short-term vs. long-term value creation and realization directly impact which contractual terms will be profitable.

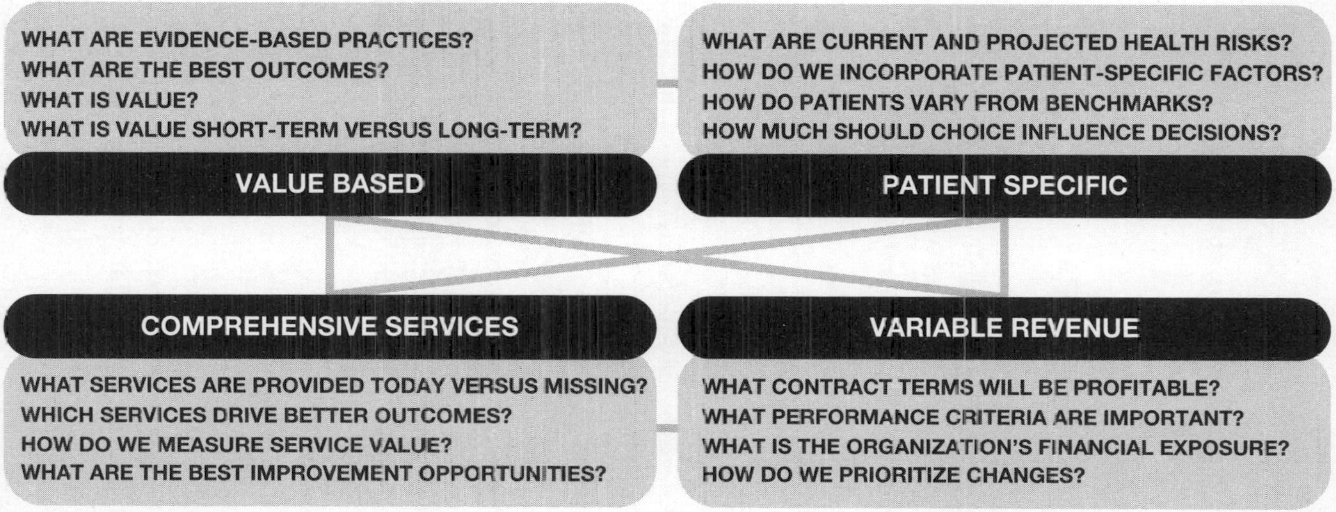

WHAT ARE CURRENT AND PROJECTED HEALTH RISKS?
HOW DO WE INCORPORATE PATIENT-SPECIFIC FACTORS?
HOW DO PATIENTS VARY FROM BENCHMARKS?
HOW MUCH SHOULD CHOICE INFLUENCE DECISIONS?

PATIENT SPECIFIC

VARIABLE REVENUE

WHAT CONTRACT TERMS WILL BE PROFITABLE?
WHAT PERFORMANCE CRITERIA ARE IMPORTANT?
WHAT IS THE ORGANIZATION'S FINANCIAL EXPOSURE?
HOW DO WE PRIORITIZE CHANGES?

WHAT ARE EVIDENCE-BASED PRACTICES?
WHAT ARE THE BEST OUTCOMES?
WHAT IS VALUE?
WHAT IS VALUE SHORT-TERM VERSUS LONG-TERM?

VALUE BASED

COMPREHENSIVE SERVICES

WHAT SERVICES ARE PROVIDED TODAY VERSUS MISSING?
WHICH SERVICES DRIVE BETTER OUTCOMES?
HOW DO WE MEASURE SERVICE VALUE?
WHAT ARE THE BEST IMPROVEMENT OPPORTUNITIES?

Figure 6.2 Shared Reimbursement Attributes.

With that as context, we can shift our attention to the specific analytical capabilities needed to answer these questions. We will briefly summarize some of these capabilities here, as the topics are covered in even more detail in subsequent chapters of the book.

WHAT IS NEEDED
Episode Case Rate Analytics (ECRA)

The concept of paying for a range of services—whether through bundled payments, comprehensive care payments, or any other mechanism—requires both providers and payers to develop more sophisticated insights into service delivery. We need to know:

- What services are typically associated with the condition?
- How much does it typically cost to deliver those services?
- How much variability exists across patients in terms of service needs?
- What risks exist in the patient population, and how should those risks be characterized?
- How does this organization compare to its peers?

Without this information, both payers and providers are flying blind in terms of profitability and risk exposures. Advanced analytics applied to episode case rates offer insights necessary for organizations to confidently enter these new contracting models; ECRA not only drives greater understanding of cost accrual, it helps each organization manage its risk exposure.

In its technical implementation, ECRA is a complex set of capabilities that combine aspects of rules engines, accounting, and clinical decision making. Beyond the typical data integration and management challenges, ECRA must account for a whole host of evolving standards and rules related to constructing episodes of care: types of care episodes, triggering events that define the start of care, boundaries around what is included within the episode of care, allocation of services, attribution of providers, and severity adjustments, just to name a few. For many patients—especially those with multiple providers and comorbidities—the construction of these models can be quite complicated. But it is being done today.

The end goal for ECRA work will be new predictive models. And whereas existing episode groupers and ECRA implementations have relied almost exclusively on claims data, future models will need to incorporate additional data: clinical data derived from EMRs and costing data (such as activity-based costing) derived from cost accounting systems. The incorporation of these additional data sources will not only improve the accuracy of the models, it will begin to drive greater consensus around the relationships between costs, services, and outcomes.

Performance Analytics

Every health organization today is coming to terms with the idea that performance will be subjected to greater scrutiny.

Industry requirements around quality reporting has led to many health organizations adopting some limited forms of performance management software, usually in the form of Web reports for metrics that influence reimbursements. Though necessary, those tools will not be sufficient for managing the growing inventory of performance-related measures—both national and contractual— for which organizations will increasingly be held accountable. And in many cases, that accountability will be public and transparent, representing increased risks for organizations not proactively managing their performance.

A few types of performance-related measures are captured in Table 6.2, and we take on the topic of performance and quality management in Chapter 12.

Risk Analytics

One of the reasons that performance management is such a critical issue is that it serves to mitigate risk. There is no escaping the fact that both providers and payers will be managing risks in new ways.

Specifically as it relates to reimbursement, a number of ideas have surfaced for how financial risks might be contained. Techniques include:

Table 6.2 Sample Performance Measures

Clinical Outcomes	Financials
Acuity measures	Fixed and variable costs
Adherence	Efficiency measures
Chronic disease prognostics	Utilization
Readmissions	Profitability
Predictive accuracy	Predictive accuracy
Quality	**Reengineering**
Quality standards	Care coordination
Safety	Preventative services
Patient satisfaction	Patient education
Physician satisfaction	Information transparency
Predictive accuracy	

- **Outlier Adjustments**—adjusting compensation for individual extreme or otherwise rare cases of care.

- **Condition and Severity Adjustments**—changing compensation based on the health context of patients.

- **Risk Corridors**—establishing standard boundaries for groups of patients beyond which compensation is adjusted.

Risk management is covered in additional detail in Chapter 11.

Value and Cost Analytics

In many ways, cost analysis—or the lack thereof—may be the biggest challenge facing health organizations.

Despite all of the discussions around health costs and novel contracting models, currently neither payer nor provider has enough cost data to make educated decisions. Providers believe that payers—through claims databases and analytical talent—are well positioned to define costs. Payers believe that providers—the people and organizations actually providing the services and incurring the costs—are in a much better position to describe costs. And both organizations are hesitant to share their own data or insights out of fear that the information will be used against them in contracting.

Chapter 8 focuses on approaches to cost and value estimation. For now, it is sufficient to say that a deeper understanding of costs is critical to both effective health policy development and sustainable business models. And the only way to get those insights is collaboration around shared data and analytics.

Health Outcomes Analytics

Once you get past all of the discussions and debates around escalating costs, the heart of an efficient and effective health and life sciences ecosystem is healthier patients. From more evidence-based decisions to care coordination to collaborative decision making, we simply must gain a better understanding of the true determinants of health outcomes.

The opportunities and goals for advanced analytics in health outcomes go far beyond applications in clinical research and population health studies. Health analytics frameworks enable practitioners to dynamically explore what happens in the real world with patients, and Chapter 7 focuses on these opportunities.

Profitability Analytics

The path to profitability looks somewhat different depending on the health sector. The business models for providers, payers, and life sciences firms—where not converged into merged entities—have very different "levers" that influence profitability. But despite their obvious differences, many of the analytical paradigms, and even the analytical models themselves, are consistent:

- **Customer Profitability Analytics.** Who are your most profitable customers? Who are your least profitable? What is the lifetime value of each customer? These questions and others are the focus of customer profitability analytics. Used commonly in other industries, these capabilities are becoming much more important in the midst of health care's restructuring. An extension of these capabilities includes contract analytics—determining which contracts and contract terms are producing the best results for the organization. These capabilities also cross over into the domain of customer analytics as well (see Chapter 10).

- **Pricing Analytics.** Health care is becoming cost competitive. Payers will increasingly steer patients to providers that offer comparable quality at lower fees. Pharmaceutical companies will increasingly face downward pricing pressures for formulary inclusion. And payers, especially those participating in the direct-to-consumer insurance markets, will be forced to compare their product and service prices against competitors. Pricing analytics can help all of these organizations optimize their pricing and incentives against revenue and costs.

- **Utilization Analytics.** Products, services, and facilities that are not used cannot drive revenue, a challenge particularly acute for providers. Utilization analytics provide insights beyond what standard reporting can offer; in addition to more accurate forecasting, predictive models can also offer insights into which initiatives and programs are effective in improving utilization. They can even be used to develop real time alerts and interventions that increase utilization.

- **Revenue Cycle Management Analytics.** Though it goes by different names in each of the market segments, the concept of revenue cycle management—ensuring complete, accurate, and timely collection of revenues—is equally applicable to each of the market segments. For payers and providers, these capabilities can directly improve reimbursement and payment practices. For life sciences companies, analytics for rebate optimization offer similar benefits.

- **Abuse Analytics.** With an estimated annual loss of more than $60 billion in the United States alone, opportunities abound in detecting and preventing fraud, waste, and abuse across the health ecosystem. Analytics-driven capabilities for the detection, recovery, and prevention of waste and abuse combine traditional business rules logic with more analytically derived capabilities such as anomaly detection, predictive modeling, and network analytics. Operating in real time, these approaches can actually detect fraud and improper payments before claims are paid.

Waste Not

Few people would argue that stopping fraud is undesirable. It is estimated that somewhere between 4% and 10% of all health benefits paid are fraudulent. So fraud is a major component of financial performance. But how do you stop it?

Comparing individual claim transactions to a database of nearly 4,000 fraud "rules" for violations is one way. But that approach has some limitations. First, it assumes the fraudulent activity has already occurred at least once, been discovered, and been coded as a rule. Second, it assumes an organization has the capacity to chase down every potential rule violation. Third, it assumes that the nature of the fraudulent activity is simple enough to be represented programmatically as a rule. And fourth, it assumes the goal is recovering monies already paid (as opposed to payment prevention).

One payer is trying a different approach. Using advanced analytical techniques such as data mining, predictive modeling, pattern recognition, and social network analysis, the organization is able to look for activities that are anomalous or containing patterns unlike peer groups. Using analytical models, the system is able to detect more sophisticated forms of fraud such as collusion between three different organizations. Much like their financial counterparts, these capabilities can be deployed in real time to stop fraudulent payments before they are ever paid.

■ **Quality and Warranty Analytics.** As health organizations evolve toward bundled payments and similar grouped cost models, care providers will, in effect, be offering a warranty on their services. If the quality is not according to the contracted specification, providers are incurring the cost and risks of remediation. This problem space has been the subject of extensive analytical models in other industries such as manufacturing and retail. Those same capabilities could also be deployed in health care to identify and fix care-related problems that contribute to lost profits.

SURVIVING AND THRIVING

There is still much to be learned about making health care financially sustainable for everyone. One of the healthiest trends recently has been the number of pilot programs provisioned to explore different models. It is only through these real-world experiences that we can develop our understanding of the right models, methods, and policies.

Across these pilot programs, though, is a disconcerting lack of advanced analytics. The ongoing focus on simple descriptive statistics is masking the fact that, even with the data we have, we don't know exactly why something is more expensive, less profitable, or used more frequently. And the natural tendency to make causal assumptions from the data—higher utilization is bad, higher costs are undesirable—puts at risk our ability to actually optimize outcomes at the right costs and service levels.

In explaining why inferential analytics are important, a statistics teacher once noted how people who buy cereal also tend to consume milk. If you were tracking the behaviors of 10,000 consumers, you might notice that, for homes that consume milk, they seem to purchase more cereal. Such a relationship, however, does not mean that milk causes cereal purchases. It also doesn't mean that cereal causes people to drink more milk at meals. And it doesn't mean that milk inflates cereal purchasing.

Without more data and more sophisticated analytical models, we run the risk of drawing incorrect conclusions from our pilot projects. It is not enough to say that costs went up or down, or that quality went up or down. We cannot accept knowing "what"—we must get to "why" and "how." We want to maximize quality at the most reasonable cost points. That is an optimization problem, and the solution requires that we delve into the causal relationships between activities, behaviors, policies, outcomes, and costs.

The insights we derive here will probably be unexpected. They will force organizations to make some tough decisions. There may be markets that become undesirable. There may be customers, products, and services that simply cannot be profitable. It may be that the time horizons for value accrual mandate different relationship contracting models and patient incentives. The point is we don't know. And we won't know until we upgrade the quality of the questions we are asking and the analytical techniques we leverage to answer them.

CASE STUDY

Is More Actually Less?

Health care providers are increasingly using analytics to justify that reimbursement for services today can prevent additional financial burdens later.

One Mid-Atlantic provider of physical therapy services analyzed 18,000 patient responses across 40 diagnoses to identify treatment patterns that consistently produced superior health outcomes. Using this data, they were able to renegotiate reimbursement contracts that were supporting suboptimal care strategies such as an inadequate number of covered therapy sessions. Though initially motivated by financial concerns, these same analytical models also provided insights into best practices in care.

In another case, a Midwestern service provider is using data from provider billing, lab, and other sources to form virtual regional health information organizations (vRHIOs) which gives providers the ability to negotiate better reimbursement terms. The vRHIO provides the data necessary to compare performance against national guidelines for evidence-based medicine. So much like an ACO, physicians are in effect incurring financial risk through clinical performance standards. This approach to financial negotiation has led to negotiated rate increases of between 15 and 20% while simultaneously driving improved health outcomes.

CHAPTER 7

Health Outcomes Analysis

NO LEECHES NECESSARY

How do we provide the best treatment the first time, every time? It seems like an impossible goal. And yet, not too long ago, effective treatment and survival of many diseases was improbable.

When the library at Alexandria was founded at the beginning of the third century BCE, medicine was still a relatively young science. Hippocrates, the father of Western medicine, lived during the century just before the library was started. The Hippocratic Corpus, a collection of his medical thoughts and teachings that included the Hippocratic Oath, may have been assembled at Alexandria.

As our understanding of medicine has grown, we have learned that characterizing disease as imbalances of body "humors" and the corresponding 2800-year-old treatment of bloodletting did not satisfy our goals of improving outcomes. Likewise, as we enter this new medical information age, we can be confident that future generations will look back and wonder how we managed to practice medicine effectively without health analytics.

ORIENTATION

Let's start by stating the obvious: a single chapter cannot cover the breadth and depth of the opportunities for clinically relevant insights attainable through health analytics. The best we can hope to accomplish in our brief tour of this topic is to give some context to how health analytics can change our understanding of medicine. We also don't want to spend time surveying the body of literature already available on health outcomes. Suffice it to say, health outcomes research is not new . . . far from it.

But from the perspective of health analytics as we have defined it (predictive, personalized, etc.), our track record on advanced analytics of health outcomes is unimpressive at best. Existing research efforts have been plagued by most if not all of the shortcomings we have already discussed, including:

- Limited use of data sources, types, and observations
- Retrospective, descriptive statistics at the exclusion of predictive models
- A focus on population-level analytics in lieu of individual differences (e.g., patient, physician, institution)
- Analyses that do not reflect real-world scope and interdependencies
- Reliance on the scientific method and empirical study to the relative exclusion of real-world explorations
- A focus on developing health policies and treatment protocol recommendations in the absence of more deeply characterizing the dynamics that ultimately influence outcomes and costs
- An inability to connect analyses to actual clinical practice

So the goal of this chapter is simply to give you a flavor for how we can overcome most of these challenges. And though we have spent the last few chapters building the case for using increasingly broader sources and types of data, we will start by focusing in on a few critical aspects of clinical data that drive a lot of what can be done in health outcomes analytics.

THE BIG SEVEN + ONE

If you are going to undertake any sort of meaningful analysis of health outcomes, there are seven data objects that drive the foundation of both analysis and interpretation. The "seven" refers to seven data dimensions that represent a patient's experience of health:

1. **Profiles**—demographic data about individual patients, physicians, departments, institutions, and geographies. Profiles include what you do, what you like, what you believe, and social connectivity (i.e., who you know, e.g., physician referral patterns) among other traits.

2. **Events**—encounters between patients and health providers, such as office visits, telemedicine consults, etc.

3. **Measures**—discrete data on all aspects of an individual—patient or provider: physical (e.g., heart rate, respiration), mental/emotional (e.g., intelligence, depression and anxiety scores), behavioral (e.g., activity levels, personality dimensions, belief scales), environmental (e.g., carcinogen exposure levels), and others. Even aspects of a patient's insurance status (i.e., insured or uninsured, deductible level) are considered measures.

4. **Diagnoses**—clinical judgments reached by health practitioners, derived from measures and often codified in electronic medical records (EMRs) and claims systems.

5. **Procedures**—protocols and activities (e.g., office and surgical procedures) executed by providers in the routine care and treatment of patients and their diagnoses.

6. **Therapies**—drugs, programs, and other interventions usually attached to a procedure that is intended to treat or cure the patient's disease.

7. **Communications**—patient-to-provider and provider-to-provider information exchanges (phone, email, meetings) regardless of context.

These seven dimensions form the basis of many analytical scenarios (see Figure 7.1). For example, "episode groupers" that have been evolving to support bundled payment models center around events

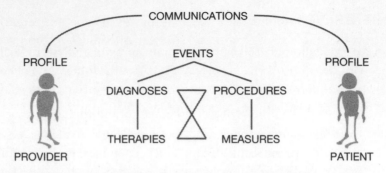

Figure 7.1 The Seven Primary Data Dimensions of Health Outcomes.

and diagnoses, linking procedures and therapies together to derive cost models. In contrast, clinical trials research usually centers around therapies and assessing their impact on measures while tightly controlling diagnoses. The rapidly evolving space of care coordination is seeking to connect communications to diagnoses, procedures, and events. Note that costs are not a separate dimension; rather, they are attributes of the other dimensions (i.e., events, procedures, therapies, etc. all have associated costs).

For our purposes here, it is not important to understand how this data is represented, or what the analytical models actually look like. The important point is that these seven core dimensions are highly reusable. If your organization can create consistent, reliable, accessible, source-agnostic information assets covering these seven dimensions, you will have a good foundation for undertaking health outcomes analytics. But there is another component of data needed.

TIMING IS EVERYTHING

A graduate school friend once told me a joke that has remained my favorite knock-knock joke of all time:

"Knock, knock."

"Who's there?"

"The Impatient Cow."

"The Impa—"

"MOOOO!"

In addition to being fun, the joke has the added benefit of requiring the joke teller to carefully understand timing, especially how timing will work for the specific person involved in the joke. If you get the timing wrong, the joke makes absolutely no sense.

In our Seven + One model, time is the " + One" component (see Figure 7.2). Earlier in the book, we said one of the challenging things about health analytics is that it requires a good characterization of time. In both health research and clinical practice, the sequence of things matters, and the time between things also matters. Looking across these disciplines, time may sometimes be:

- An Assumption—we might assume that patients who contract infections within 1 week after surgery are experiencing an avoidable medical complication
- A Determinant of Outcomes—we might find that antibiotic doses twice daily are more effective than doses once a day (i.e., time is a variable of therapies and procedures)

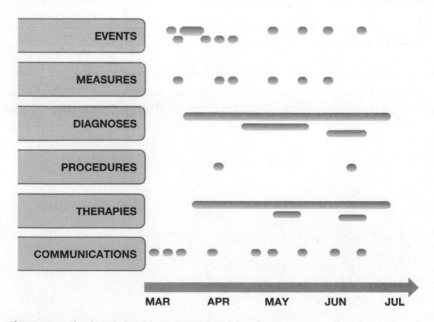

Figure 7.2 Time's Relationship to the Dimensions of HOA.

■ An Outcome—we might find that patients who received antibiotics more frequently spent less time in the hospital (i.e., time is a measure)

Of course, it is not at all uncommon for time to be important in analytics of all types. What makes time a little different in health analytics is how frequently "time as an assumption" surfaces, and how important that dimension becomes in making inferences or drawing conclusions. So, like costs, time is technically an attribute of the seven major data dimensions, but because its role in assumptions and research designs is so foundational, we call it out separately as its own domain.

Each of our seven data dimensions exists in the context of time (see Figure 7.3). Patients don't see just one provider; over time, they see multiple providers, often in direct correlation to diagnoses. Patients have many events, diagnoses, procedures, therapies, and measures. The assumptions we make in analyzing the data depend on when events, diagnoses, and therapies occur in relation to each other. In short, in order for us to draw conclusions from the data, we have to somehow associate individual data items together. That concept is called grouping.

GROUPERS

As a class of software, episode groupers have evolved into one of the more important capabilities within a health enterprise. Episode groupers initially focused on processing claims data. By grouping claims

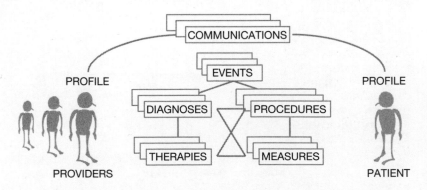

Figure 7.3 Data Dimensions Include Multiple Data Points Over Time.

together, analysts could determine things like how much a given condition typically costs to treat, and how individual providers perform against the norm. From this data, the industry is moving forward with bundled payment models (a topic we explored briefly in Chapter 6).

Grouping sounds simple, but it is actually a very complicated process consisting of both methodologies and rules. Comorbidities, medical complications, risk adjustments, and many other issues must be factored into the grouping process. The methodologies, rules, and assumptions for grouping logic are typically derived from accepted standards of clinical practice, expert opinion, and national standards established by government agencies among other sources. In addition, grouper software typically includes the facility to add custom groupers to an implementation.

As we will see in subsequent chapters, the choice of episode grouper may actually determine a lot about how health businesses perform. For now, it is sufficient to acknowledge that grouping logic is critical to linking our data together into clinically meaningful and statistically consistent episodes of care.[1]

THE POPULATION-PATIENT PIVOT

Now that we have our data assets in a more usable structure, our journey toward better health outcomes through analytics can begin.

As a discipline, health outcomes research has historically focused largely on population health. There are several reasons for this. First, there has been a belief that addressing health issues at the population level also addresses the main issues at the individual level. Second, much of health outcomes research has been in support of policy development—by definition, a population-focused area. Third, the only way historically to get sufficient electronic information from which to draw meaningful conclusions was to look at populations. And fourth, it has always been assumed that the physician, as the final mediator-of-care decisions, would exercise whatever personalization in clinical practice required to address the needs of each individual patient.

But in a more modern conceptualization of health outcomes research, many of these propositions do not hold true. We have access to much more data about individuals. We know that no single individual reflects the dynamics of a population. We know that, regardless of policy development and standardization of care, variability in care can be a very positive force (or a very negative one).

As such, our view of health outcomes analytics involves three guiding principles:

1. **The definition of a "population" should be analytically derived.** When we arbitrarily define populations based on single medical conditions (e.g., all diabetics, all COPD patients, etc.), we are making an assumption that the single medical condition stratification is the most meaningful. But that is not necessarily true. Analytics can inform us on how patients stratify, segment, and cluster. And we should use that information to drive our decision-making process.

2. **There is no ultimate distinction between population and individual health outcomes.** Every individual patient exists in multiple populations simultaneously (see Figure 7.4). For example, an expectant mother on the maternity ward is a member of the female population. She might also hold memberships in the Hispanic, Diabetic, and High-Blood-Pressure populations. Assuming she does, she also holds memberships in the Diabetic-Hispanic, Female-High-Blood-Pressure, Hispanic-High-Blood-Pressure, and Female-Hispanic-Diabetic-High-Blood-Pressure populations (among many others). All of these populations are not only acceptable in analytics, but they are the proper units of population study. Some population stratifications may not be relevant; for example, maybe Female-High-Blood-Pressure and Female-Hispanic-Diabetic-High-Blood-Pressure experience health similarly. Other population stratifications may be critically important—it may be that some factor present in Hispanic females with diabetes and high blood pressure correlates with a dramatically elevated risk factor. Of course, at some point you reach a population of one, which will always be the last mile that a physician must travel. But since there is no hard-and-fast way of saying how many patients make a population, it is more useful to assume that any collection of patients is composed of multiple populations. Our goal should

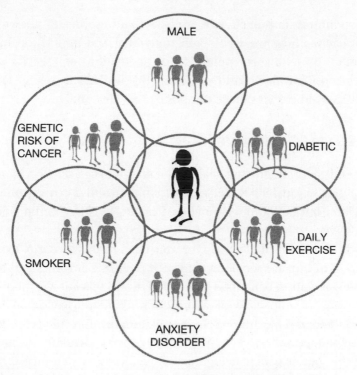

Figure 7.4 Patients Exist Simultaneously in Many Overlapping Populations.

be to determine each patient's significant population memberships, and then to use that information to drive care decisions—
both by using treatments that are effective for each population,
and also treatments shown to be effective for patients who share
similar population memberships.

3. **Physicians should be able to pivot between population-
oriented views and individual-oriented views of health
outcomes analysis.** There is value in looking at "what is
generally true." There is also value in looking at "what is likely
true for this patient." The data and analytical algorithms are the
same. So providers, payers, researchers, and others need to be
able to switch between these two views of health in order to
make the most educated and informed decisions regarding
health outcomes.

So with our improved data assets, we can use health analytics to recharacterize how we study both individual and population health dynamics. By letting our definition of populations emerge from the data, we position ourselves to see a deeper view of health-related factors and risks. And we set ourselves up for predictive analytics.

PATIENTS LIKE THIS ONE

If our end goal of improving health outcomes is to be achieved, we need to apply these capabilities. The application to health outcomes research is obvious, but how can we move this capability closer to the point of care delivery?

One idea is called Patients Like This One. In this scenario, existing standards of care are supplemented with real-time analytics that facilitate the population-patient pivot. An analytical application (as shown in Figure 7.5) is supplied with information about the condition being treated, and is able to present population-level results of various treatment approaches. Then, by providing the application information about the specific patient being treated, predictive models project likely outcomes of each treatment alternative based on patients that resemble this particular patient (i.e., patients that share similar population memberships or factors).

Another idea concerns directing provider and payer resources toward higher-risk factors. The basic question being answered is "What are the factors that are most likely to influence health outcomes?" This analysis uses more than just information about the patient—it incorporates data regarding the physician, organization, maturity of clinical evidence, and any other dimensions available that correlate with positive or negative results.

In Figure 7.6, a patient's overall health outcome projection is below average (the center line). So what is contributing to that potentially negative outcome? Is it the attending physician? Do we not know enough about the disease progression? The example shows that three categories of factors—patient, evidence, and financial—are contributing to that lower projected outcome, and the most significant negative factors are the patient-specific factors. By drilling in to those factors to see which ones are elevating the risk, providers and payers can institute

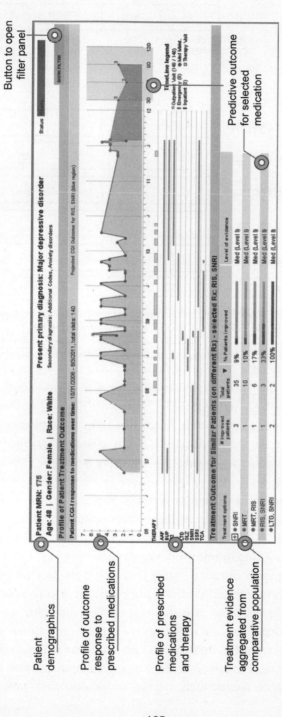

Figure 7.5 An Example of a Health Outcomes Analytics Application.
Source: Ketan Mane, PhD, Senior Research Scientist at RENCI, University of North Carolina at Chapel Hill. Used with permission.

105

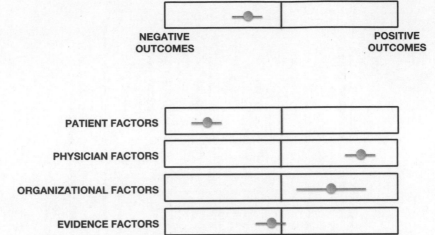

Figure 7.6 Relative Contributions to Health Risk Factors.

interventional, preventative, and patient engagement strategies targeted to improve the patient's prognosis.

Note that this model need not be used as a one-time, manual exercise. As we look to incorporate more real-time information feeds into our health delivery system, outcomes and risk assessments can be run in real time. As patient data feeds begin to show a trajectory toward elevated risk, health providers can be notified in order to introduce interventions.

For example, if a patient is given a prescription for a drug, our predictive models may show that patients that fit this particular patient's profile often fail to get their prescriptions filled (e.g., lower socioeconomic status, unmarried, does not own a car, limited insurance). So our model can set a trigger that says if an electronic prescription claim is not detected with 72 hours, notify a care coordination team within the primary care facility to follow up with the patient, engaging supplemental care resources (i.e., home prescription delivery, prescription payment assistance) to improve the patient's predicted health outcomes. Primary care facilities, particularly those affiliated with patient-centered medical homes or accountable care delivery models, can begin to triage day-to-day work based on managing outcomes—imagine a real-time scoreboard that shows a list of patients, ranked high-to-low in terms of interventional urgency.

ONE MODEL, MANY BENEFICIARIES

Though we've focused our discussion on analytical applications primarily benefiting individual patients, could our health outcomes analyses benefit other constituencies as well?

The National Collaborative for Bio-Preparedness (NCB-Prepared) has demonstrated one such example. NCB-Prepared is a public-private partnership focused on improving syndromic surveillance through nontraditional sources of data, advanced analytics, and cloud computing. By focusing on several of our Seven + One data dimensions—profiles, communications, and time—the partnership has been able to show that they could detect and predict the propagation of public health threats such as communicable diseases weeks or months before the progression actually occurs. How? By using data mining and predictive modeling on data sets that would not otherwise be merged, such as ambulance calls, hospital admissions, and social media data freely provided by consumers. In essence, they can see, amplify, and verify otherwise weak signals occurring in the real world.

If you could predict, for example, the spread of a communicable disease across a state, what might you do with that capability?

- Raise public awareness of health interventions, such as hand washing
- Increase medical responder and provider readiness
- Improve retailer stocks of medicines and supplies
- Provide better mobilization and situational awareness for federal, state, and local resources managing catastrophic issues such as bioterrorism

In short, many of the analytical models we can and should build are not about benefiting one single market or constituent. Rather, the insights should be used across a broad range of constituencies: patients, providers, emergency responders, researchers, policy makers, retailers, national security defenders, and many more.

The examples above are just the tip of the iceberg. As illustrated in Table 7.1, by selecting any one of our dimensions as a focus, you can begin to envision a whole portfolio of predictive and advanced analytical applications that can drive more effective health outcomes. Analytics can help us determine what a "patient like this one" actually looks like—what is significant in understanding this particular patient or patient population?

Table 7.1 Data Dimensions and Sample Questions

Focus Dimension	Example Advanced Analytical Questions
Profile	■ What personal factors influence a patient's likelihood to proactively engage around their health? ■ How do the health outcomes obtained by individual physicians vary by organizational affiliation? ■ How and why do certain physician relationships (e.g., referral patterns) produce different health outcomes for patients?
Communications	■ What factors modulate the effectiveness of medical communications? ■ What is the optimal timing of communications across the various communication channels (e.g., phone, email, etc.)? ■ What individual differences can be fine-tuned to improve the effectiveness of patient-provider communications?
Events	■ What factors influence the comparative effectiveness of telemedicine encounters in comparison to face-to-face? ■ What is the optimal balance between the frequency of preventative medicine encounters and effective preventative care? ■ How can we use existing patterns of health-related events for early detection and intervention of health threats—reducing the size, scope, duration, and impact?
Diagnoses	■ What diagnoses are most frequently missed on the first encounter, and what factors influence misdiagnosis? ■ How long does it take to diagnose a condition, and what factors influence earlier diagnosis and treatment? ■ How do diagnoses move through time, and what do those movements tell us about the disease and treatments?
Procedures	■ What factors interact with which variations in treatment to influence outcomes? ■ How does the time between procedures influence outcomes? ■ How do specific procedures impact risks?

(continued)

Table 7.1 (*Continued*)

Therapies	▪ What factors most significantly determine the comparative effectiveness of different treatments? ▪ What research designs demonstrate the comparative effectiveness of a drug class more quickly and cost effectively? ▪ What combination of drugs and other therapies will likely produce the best benefits with the least risks and adverse experiences for this particular patient?
Measures	▪ What measures most reliably predict disease manifestation and/or progression? ▪ What can the covariations within a broader set of measures tell us about the underlying causes and dynamics of diseases? ▪ Which factors most reliably predict a patient's ultimate experience of health for a given condition?

THE ROLE OF RULES ENGINES

One thing that will be evident as you look at Table 7.1 is that answering these questions is way beyond the capabilities of traditional health care rules engines. Typical clinical decision support applications—usually driven by a library of if-then statements (i.e., if this is true, then suggest or do that)—absolutely have a role to play in ensuring good care delivery. But in the future of medicine, the role of rules engines should be as an adjunct to a more data-driven approach to health outcomes (e.g., as a quality control measure), not as guidance for clinical practice.

The conditional clauses that end up in rules engines are rarely (if ever) the product of a predictive analysis. They typically reflect opinion on preferred clinical practices, or widely acknowledged adverse situations to avoid. Accordingly, rules engines usually suffer from three shortcomings:

1. **What is a rule?** The lines get "fuzzy" around what should be implemented in a rules engine. Clearly defined boundaries such as contraindicated medications are obvious. But as you move toward implementing clinical practices in rules engines, all sorts of potential conflicts emerge. At the root of the conflict is the fact that rules are binary: true or false. But the practice of medicine is anything but binary.

2. **Rules engines do not dynamically learn and adapt to what is happening in the real world.** Not only does their binary nature preclude variability in practice, those variations in practice are not used to inform subsequent decision making.

3. **How long can we wait?** The inevitable implementation delays—the time between industry discussions and decisions about a rule definition, and that rule's subsequent availability in software—contribute to the gaps in quality and health outcomes.

Given our discussion of the many factors that should be accounted for in health analytics, consider the ramifications of using rules engines to accomplish this. If you tried to manually describe, codify, maintain, and manage the universe of rules associated with all of the different populations, diseases, measures, procedures, and therapies, it would be an unattainable, unsustainable task. In contrast, analytical models work from data, whatever that data might be. Whether a negative outcome is predicted from a single factor or a dozen, it doesn't make any difference. And as evolving forces in the real world adjust a patient's predicted outcomes, the analytical models can improve and adapt. In short, if you want an active learning health system, advanced analytics are a requirement.

CHALLENGES IN HEALTH OUTCOMES ANALYTICS

So the opportunity and benefits for advanced analytics in health outcomes analysis are clear. What stops people from doing it? We've covered a few of the more significant limitations in our earlier chapters on analytics and data, but it is worth recapping some of the more significant challenges.

Characterizing Clinical Context

Many of our clinical systems are getting good at capturing, collecting, organizing, and storing clinical data and records. But even in systems that represent best-of-breed today, from an analytics perspective we often lack the right information.

Taking this out of the clinical environment for a moment, if I were to send you a one-word message—"Fire"—how would you interpret that? You can't interpret it without more information. If you know I am an emergency responder, you might assume I am communicating that something is burning. If you know that my hobby is alchemy, you might assume I am talking about one of the four basic elements of the alchemical universe. And if you know I am an emergency responder who has a hobby of alchemy, but I am presently deployed in a war zone as a gunnery sergeant, your conclusion will probably be different still.

Every aspiring journalist learns the critical six questions: who, what, when, where, why, and how. In many cases, our systems only collect a fraction of this information. We may know a single aspect of the what (e.g., respiration rate), but not the bulk of the what (e.g., was this taken before, during, or after a physical stress test). We may know who and when, but have no visibility into the why or how. We may know the measure is "9," but we may not know that "9" was corrected to "19" after we brought the data in for analysis, or that the units were recorded wrong, or that the value is considered out of range for this setting. Increasingly, metadata—information about our information—is important in conducting analyses and drawing conclusions.

There are many ways to get more metadata. Ideally, systems are designed to ask, collect, and structure sufficient metadata to provide context later. When that doesn't happen, we can sometimes re-create metadata after the fact by going back to the source—the research or treatment protocol used, for example. In some cases, we can derive metadata from other data in the record or another data source. Or in the worst case, we can make explicit assumptions about the context, and then limit how broadly we interpret our results to respect the assumptions we made.

Clinical context and the use of metadata is a very broad and important topic in information sciences (if you really want to take on a thought experiment, consider that one person's data can be another person's metadata, and vice versa). For now, just remember it's not just the data we need—we also need the data about the data.

Master Data Management

In Chapter 4, we mentioned that inconsistencies in how we collect data across systems cause challenges for analytics. If a given patient's name, unique identifier, and other information are different based on institution, division, department, and software system, it becomes difficult to merge data for purposes of analyses. These inconsistencies also create risks of errors and inefficiencies in workflow that elevate the costs of care.

In other industries, master data management has emerged as a discipline focused on solving this problem. The basic idea is that institutions should have certain data objects—master data—that are managed as common assets for purposes of quality, consistency, and efficiency. Common master data objects include company names, billing addresses, people names, reference data, and many others. In health care, master patient identifiers (MPIs) are one limited form of master data management concepts, though the discipline is much more sophisticated than assigning one unique number across systems.

Master data management impacts three of the seven vectors of information management discussed in Chapter 3; namely, data governance, data quality, and data integration. So it is a very important topic. Health institutions that lack master data management strategies will increasingly feel the costs and delays associated with rising data volumes of inconsistent quality and utility.

Consistency in Enterprise Calculations

If you've ever had the experience of configuring options on a new car, you know how important bundling can be. Your desired car may have a base price of $35,000, and you may only want heated seats and a sunroof. But if those two options (which should retail at around $1000 separately) are only purchased in feature bundles with prerequisites, your $35,000 car can rapidly become a $45,000 car. The grouping of features and costs has a dramatic impact on the actual costs incurred, and must be factored in when determining budget, financing, etc. If you use a different approach than what the car dealer used, your math is not going to work.

Similarly, it is very important that the methodologies we use for health outcomes analysis are the same ones we use in exploring costs, risks, reimbursement, and contracting strategies. Earlier in this chapter we discussed groupers—logic that allows us to link data together into clinically meaningful and statistically consistent episodes of care. In health outcomes analysis, these groupers form a foundational element of how we are assessing and improving care.

If different grouping logic is used elsewhere within the institution—for example, if reimbursement and contracting are using a different approach for assessing costs and risks—we may end up contracting for something very different than what we are delivering. If our vision of connecting health outcomes, risks, and costs into more unified models is to come to fruition, our methodologies need to be consistent across these different business domains. This is another reason why health analytics must be an enterprise-level competency: we need to make assumptions explicitly and consistently, and we need to apply improvements uniformly.

HEALTH OUTCOMES ANALYTICS IN PRACTICE

So how can these models be applied in a clinical context? Should providers start pulling up data visualization tools in front of patients? Are physicians supposed to become data scientists? The answer to these questions is likely no in both cases, though individuals and institutions will differ.

When we discussed information consumption in Chapter 3, we mentioned that there are multiple ways of exposing analytical insights. In this chapter, we make no assumptions about clinical workflow implications or specific implementation strategies. We expect these capabilities to be used across a broad spectrum of business and scientific scenarios, including clinical research, financial modeling, disease management, and yes, even care delivery. The right question to ask is, "If you had this capability, what would you do with it?" The ideas and options will be many and varied. And as organizations learn and mature in the discipline of health analytics, those ideas will drive a whole new generation of software.

The real challenge in health outcomes analytics is not about the workflow, and it is not technical. The real underlying question is one of clinical risk taking. Today, treatment risks are basically shared—since the industry uses consensus to determine clinical best practices, the risks around an individual practitioner's decision making is in effect distributed throughout the industry. If a standardized clinical decision became litigated, for example, an army of experts could testify that the practitioner used accepted standards of clinical care.

What if individual practitioners were able to discover treatment improvements without conducting controlled clinical research? What role does industry consensus serve in a model where practitioners are empowered with real-world data? Should providers, for example, be able to save each patient-specific analysis they conduct to inform each care decision they make so that the decision can be defended later if needed? What are the rules of ethics—if providers conduct analyses and see trends not represented in standardized treatments, are they ethically bound to adjust their practice? What is the right balance of control between standardized clinical practices and real-world evidence-informed practice, especially when there is a significant time delay between aligning those two things? Can the risk of litigation be mitigated by putting more information in front of patients, and explicitly engaging in more shared decision making on the potential benefits and risks?

These are all very important questions. And yet, here is the truth before us: practitioners are already practicing medicine by independent discovery. They select drugs and treatments that have worked well for them in the past. They use alternate indications for drugs. They exercise clinical judgment through the art of medicine. The question is whether you want that art and judgment informed by data. As you will see in Chapter 13, health analytics are leading to the democratization of research, and new models of reaching consensus on best practices. But it will take time for the new democracy to learn how to govern.

THE MARVELOUS LEECH

Though bloodletting as a therapy does not offer the panacea of therapeutic value we once thought it did, leeches themselves actually do carry some medical innovation. The worms are still seen to offer therapeutic value in reconstructive and microsurgeries where blood-related challenges exist. Leech saliva contains a protein called hirudin, an anticoagulant that helps the leech keep the blood supply flowing. Hirudin can help with a wide variety of medical issues, including blood coagulation disorders, blood clots, skin hematomas, and varicose veins. And as you might imagine, for patients who are allergic to heparin, hirudin can be a very important treatment. As leeches are quite small, it would be difficult to generate hirudin in sufficient volumes for clinical treatment. But technology—in this case, recombinant DNA—has enabled us to surpass the biological limitations of the small worms, thereby unlocking the value of hirudin for patients. Technology allows us to overcome the limitations of humans as well. Health complexity may exceed human cognition, but it doesn't exceed human creativity.

Fact or Fiction?

CASE STUDY

Some industry professionals still believe that the idea of improving care using analytics on clinical data is pure fiction. Is anyone actually doing this?

Consider the case of a U.S. bone marrow transplant center. Aggregating more than a decade's worth of patient data, practitioners use a health analytics environment to predict patient outcomes under specific treatment protocols. Care teams use the system during weekly care coordination sessions to assist in collaborative decision making. One of the physician leaders describes this analytical capability as "statistical support for actual patient care decisions on a real-time basis."

As the capability matured, the center has found that the same analytical assets can be leveraged for multiple uses. For example, the environment supports new research programs, serving both as a research data pool as well as a means of answering questions by review boards. The environment also provides a valuable tool used in teaching, enabling students to ask and answer novel questions about health outcomes probabilities. And the system directly supports the organization's clinical quality goals, continually monitoring patients and their corresponding conditions, and comparing those patients to expected conditions, treatments, and outcomes.

NOTE

1. As an aside, it can be argued that episode grouper logic is also an implementation of hypotheses—the hypothesis being that this set of human-derived rules and logic is the best characterization. Though we do not discuss this topic, it is important to note that, in the future, grouper logic itself can and should be the subject of analytical inquiry (e.g., segmentation, optimization).

CHAPTER **8**

Health Value
and Cost

AN ASYMMETRICAL INDUSTRY

What is the real relationship between health outcomes, costs, and sustainable value? Today we struggle in answering that question due to limitations of our human knowledge, misalignment of incentives, and consensus on how "value" can translate into standardized, efficient processes (both business and medical). Like it or not, medicine is a business, so the question is do we actually know how to run it efficiently?

If there were two terms that have dominated the discussions of health reform, those words would be "cost" and "value." And to the casual observer, some inherent aspects of the industry today do not seem intuitive from a business perspective. The asymmetrical nature of the economic and information models inherent in the health ecosystem mean that the consumer of the industry's products and services (i.e., patients):

- Are not the decision makers in product and service selection (i.e., providers);

- Are not the entity that pays for those products and services (i.e., payers);

- Are not directly guiding future product/service direction (i.e., researchers, life sciences firms);

- Do not have much facility for evaluating prduct and service quality.

117

Adding insult to injury, both providers and insurers can hold near monopolies in some geographies, and the price of products and services depends on who is paying.

From an economic perspective, a lot of these issues are unhealthy. They create an environment where the otherwise-balance-tending forces of economic value are not working properly. The Institute of Medicine's estimated industry waste of $750 billion each year is largely attributable to a market not structured around value. And whereas conservative advocates would argue that government involvement in health care drives this same type of imbalance, no set of policy decisions—regardless of political stance—could be effective in righting a market so fraught with asymmetries. The challenges are much more fundamental.

Virtually no one would argue that existing reforms are sufficient to deal with the overall health crisis, as they do nothing to address one simple question: What should the right health care cost? To answer that value-oriented question, you need at least three pieces of information:

1. What is the "right health care"?
2. How much does that product/service cost to produce?
3. How much value does the care deliver?

For this chapter, we characterize value as a derivative of a complex set of interrelationships between people and processes as shown in Figure 8.1. Across these interrelationships, we believe three fundamental issues encourage or inhibit the attainment of reasonable value:

1. **Knowledge.** Do we know where the costs are? Do we know what treatments will be effective? Do we understand how diseases actually progress, and how we prevent them? Do we know what matters?

2. **Incentives.** Are we motivated to undertake behaviors that avoid costs for everyone? That avoid the occurrence of medical conditions? That drive the design of and efficiency within the system? Are we steered toward what matters?

3. **Values.** Do we agree what the "right" thing is? As individuals, do we prioritize outcomes and their associated costs similarly enough to get scale and efficiency through standardization?

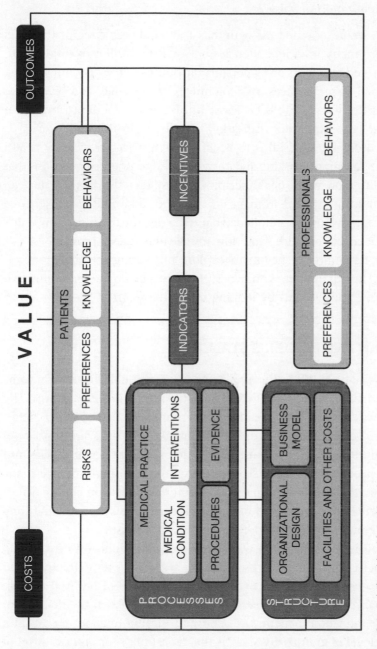

Figure 8.1 Relationships in Health Value.

Are our beliefs, preferences, and behaviors consistent with the realization of value?

Any value-oriented dialogue has to include all three of these, as there are many interdependencies between them. For example, both patients and providers bring personal attributes to the decision-making table such as preferences, risk tolerances, knowledge, and behavioral propensities (see Figure 8.1). Those attributes have a direct impact on both the perception and realization of value in health care.

Accordingly, our goal is to begin to paint a picture of how health analytics can support asking and answering value-oriented questions that will yield a more viable health sector. Our position is that health value can and should be derived from health analytics that address those three questions previously mentioned: what is the right health care? how much should it cost to produce? and how much value does it provide?

We have already begun to explore answering the first question through health outcomes analytics. Now we take up the remaining two questions, and we start by looking inside the math of "health value."

KAPLAN AND PORTER'S STAND

In September of 2011, *Harvard Business Review* published a very compelling article called "How to Solve the Cost Crisis in Health Care." The article was penned by two giants in the management and health fields: Michael Porter, author of the groundbreaking book *Redefining Health Care*; and Robert Kaplan, author of countless management articles and architect of the "balanced scorecard" approach to performance management. If either of these men had written an article on boiling water, most people like me would have read it eagerly. So the idea that they would come together to address health was fantastic.

Their recommendation was reasonably simple: health care should get a better grasp of costs by adopting a specific methodology called "activity-based costing" (ABC). This approach could be used to help define and improve the time and costs associated with the delivery of care for individual patients, as opposed to trying to allocate costs at a higher level of granularity such as the department- or practice-level of health providers.

What is ABC? In general, ABC is a costing methodology that assigns costs to organizational activities based on the consumption of resources within that activity. In other words, ABC looks at organizational processes and enumerates how costs actually accrue. Kaplan and Porter's proposal was actually to use a specific form of ABC called time-driven activity-based costing, a slightly more efficient and cost-effective approach to implementing the methodology (though the distinction in the methods are not important at the moment).

Kaplan and Porter were not the first people to recommend implementing ABC in health care, but they have been two visible proponents of the approach. The balancing act for health organizations is related to return on investment. ABC can be expensive and time-consuming to implement, especially in highly matrixed environments. Nevertheless, ABC enables provider organizations to characterize costs, the second of our questions previously mentioned. But ABC does not answer the third question: what is the actual value?

THE ELUSIVE HEALTH VALUE

In making their ABC recommendation, Kaplan and Porter first had to actually define "health value."

Porter has arguably been the most prolific writer on health value in the United States, and many people prior to Kaplan and Porter have tried to define health value.[1] It is a tricky business. Acknowledging the obvious complexities inherent in the health ecosystem, Porter and others have nevertheless set forth four primary components to a health value approach:

1. A definition of health value, which is patient outcomes achieved per dollar spent.

2. A six-level health-outcomes hierarchy that defines how the value "numerator" of #1 is derived.

3. A health-costing approach based on time-driven activity-based costing that defines how the "denominator" of #1 is derived.

4. A "chain of causality" that produces those outcomes, attempting to account for initial patient conditions, care process, and health indicators, among other things.

In essence, Kaplan and Porter argue that one way to derive value is to add up all the weighted outcomes and divide by the real accrued costs, and you get value. It is an elegant and simple concept, and it is difficult to argue with the logic. Most consumers would agree with the idea that the value they get from something is a comparison of what they get versus what it costs. Products and services that deliver good "outcomes" (e.g., pleasure, money, safety, security, etc.) for a reasonable cost to the consumer are considered a good value.

Now, at the beginning of this book, we said we would not be focusing on mathematics. But for the sake of discussing value, we are going to bend that rule for a few moments, as the math actually helps us understand the challenges in deriving value.

In mathematical terms, you could express the proposed calculation of value in the following formula:

$$V_t = \frac{\sum (o_n \times f_n)}{\sum c_z}$$

where:

- V is a measure of overall health value
- o is each specific health outcome measure;
- f is a patient-oriented weighting factor associated with each outcome measure;
- c is each specific cost measure;
- n represents a variable number of itemized outcome measures;
- z represents a variable number of costs; and
- t represents a point in time where value assessment is occurring (with overall value assessed in aggregate).

So the formula simply states that if you add up ($\sum$) all of the outcomes (o) and how important they are (f), and you divide that by the sum ($\sum$) of all of the costs (c), you get the value (V).

Considerable discussion in the industry has been devoted to o and c in our equation above—how do you conceptualize an outcome, and how should you assign a cost? Some of the challenges in understanding these two factors include:

- **Outcome Modeling**—defining meaningful and consistent outcome endpoints that represent the outcomes significant to providers and patients.

- **Episode Grouping**—defining the collection of events, treatments, and other factors that define the episode of care being evaluated (see Chapter 7 for more information on this).

- **Comorbidities and Risks**—defining the roles of concurrent medical issues and how those conditions should be factored in to each calculation of value.

- **Institutional Variation on Structuring and Cost Allocations**—defining parameters for the actual accrual of costs that are reasonably consistent across provider settings.

With time, effort, and collaboration, each of these issues can be overcome. In many cases, the solution is as simple as putting a "stake in the ground" for something that is defensible. In a proverbial desert of real-world information on these topics, any water is good water; ice and fancy glasses can be acquired later.

DISSECTING VALUE

So, we need to know three variables to calculate health value: the list of outcomes we want (o), the weighting for each outcome (f), and the costs accrued in getting those outcomes (c). Let's explore briefly each of these variables and how analytics might help us to characterize value.

The Outcomes We Want (o)

We devoted an earlier chapter to exploring how health analytics can serve the needs of health outcomes analysis. Beyond the specific issues we looked at such as safety and efficacy, we actually have a broader set of needs around outcomes.

One of the challenges in systematically assessing health outcomes is the lack of a consistent taxonomy for even defining health outcomes. As a matter of routine practice, health outcomes assessment is highly variable in its implementation, even in the more empirical applications such as routine patient health assessments. "What is important?" varies by disease, assessment instrument, treatment protocol, goal of the assessment, and many other factors.

One reason for this variability is confusion between the o and the f in our formula. In the face of patient-, provider-, and disease-specific inconsistencies, the industry's approach has been to accept variability in articulating outcomes—we let the f's change our o's.

Yet in reality, there are probably a reasonably finite number of health outcomes that matter to both patients and providers, and that are applicable regardless of disease. Table 8.1 describes a sample of common health outcomes that should be measured as part of calculating health value.

Though there will always be unique attributes of patients, providers, and diseases, a more consistent expression of health outcomes enables us to more effectively unlock the opportunities in using advanced analytics. As Table 8.1 suggests, the question is not "if" these outcome measures are important. Rather, the question is "how important" is each outcome in this particular case, for this particular patient, at this time, with this provider. Acknowledging that they are all important, it is clear that our current practice of assessing reasonably insular dimensions of health outcomes with patients—customer satisfaction, for example, or functional status—retrospectively and in a somewhat *ad hoc* way does not really represent outcomes. Patients experience outcomes more holistically, so we should assess it accordingly.

Though our earlier chapter on health outcomes analysis focused mainly on the clinical dimensions of care decisions, a more

Table 8.1 Sample Outcomes Measures

Clinical	Financial/Administrative	Personal
▪ Survival	▪ Affordable expenses	▪ Quality of life improvement
▪ Cure	▪ Cost risk avoidance	▪ Congruence with belief
▪ Reduce suffering	▪ Reimbursement	systems
▪ Health maintenance	coverage	▪ Functional status (e.g., return
▪ Control disease	▪ Availability of financial	to sports)
progression	assistance	▪ Length of inpatient treatment
▪ Risk avoidance	▪ Customer satisfaction	

comprehensive approach to health outcomes is one that acknowledges our need to connect health outcomes to value, and therefore
includes a richer representation of the various outcomes and alternatives. And it should cover treatments, as well as interventional and
preventative activities.

Outcome Weighting (f)

The real Achilles heel of value measurement is that sneaky little f—the
weighting. Why? Because it produces a paradox:

> *We need standards of care, evidence-based practice, and consistency
> in defining and implementing value-based structures*

but

> *We are willing to accept variability (potentially high) in the
> prioritization of health outcomes (and therefore the definition and
> realization of health value).*

Note that the core of this issue is not whether patients should be at
the center of value articulation—of course they should be. The core of
the issue is that providers, payers, and patients cannot agree how
relatively important a particular health outcome might be. Do all
providers believe the same outcome for a patient is equally important?
Do all patients value a particular outcome equally? Do patients and
providers always agree on the importance? The answer to all three of
these questions is a definitive no.

Some outcomes are clear: death, for example, is usually a bad
outcome. Others are not quite so clear. Is an elderly patient's ability
to gain sufficient mobility for independent living after a surgery important? Maybe. Are they already in an assisted—living facility? Do they
plan to be? How would they feel about it?

The formula assumes patients express rational, consistent health
preferences and behaviors—but they often don't. It assumes providers
consistently make objective, evidence-based decisions—but they often
don't. It assumes payers make decisions based on long-term patient
benefit rather than short-term cost containment—but they often don't.
The business utility of the value metric V is only as strong as the clarity

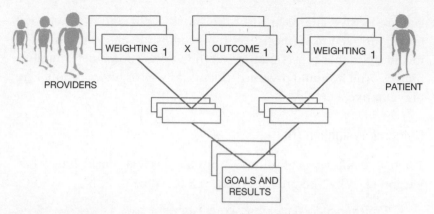

Figure 8.2 Health Outcomes and Weighting for Both Providers and Patients.

on the inputs into the equation (both numerator and denominator), and unfortunately, even if we could agree on the list of outcome measures, we may not agree on the weighting of those measures (see Figure 8.2).

Does this mean the formula is useless? Not at all! It just means that we need to account for the variability that we expect to see in the value calculations. We need to accept that the calculation of value requires a more sophisticated methodology than policies and clinical guidelines can easily provide. In short, value is subjective as well as objective.

Costs (c)

For a wide variety of reasons—contracting, profitability, reimbursement, merger financials—health institutions are increasingly accepting that historical approaches to cost analysis are woefully inadequate.

Providers have garnered much of the attention in cost analysis, and with good reason. But it is important to acknowledge that the other market segments need better costing information as well. Pharmaceutical companies cannot continue to write blank checks for research programs with uncertain futures, or pursue sales and marketing initiatives without an understanding of the impacts to profitability. Health plans that cannot figure out how to efficiency manage care and reimbursement, particularly while maintaining customer satisfaction and a positive consumer perception, will not be competitive in a consumer-driven, price-conscious health insurance market. The rising costs associated with increasing information volumes and the demand for reengineering can only be stemmed by discriminating decision making informed around costs and benefits; without the "costs" part, no one can make a good business decision.

By now, it should be clear that we have to set aside the notion that change programs within any one market segment, though important components of change, are sufficient in isolation to drive the needed transformation. And if we can accept that the rising costs of health care are unsustainable, then one aspect of the solution should be self-evident: you cannot improve what you do not measure. The question is not "if" a health institution should undertake a more rigorous costing methodology; rather, the question is "how."

Activity-Based Costing

Kaplan and Porter's premise was that ABC would provide better visibility to how costs actually accrue. Any objective evaluation of costing approaches would likely conclude that ABC has a number of strongly desirable characteristics in dealing with health-related costing: it provides a low level of granularity in cost assignment, it works well in dealing with complex processes, and it distinguishes between different types of costs (e.g., fixed, variable, overhead) that are important to health economics and industry transformation.

Ironically, the biggest challenge to generally using ABC is the cost of implementing it. The methodology and level of detail involved can take a lot of effort to put in place, especially in organizational environments that lack sophisticated information technologies that can automate some of the data collection. The cost criticism of ABC has led Kaplan and others to develop the modified approach called "time-driven activity-based costing" (TDABC) that they actually propose for health care. The intended cost mitigation of TDABC is still the subject of debate and speculation, especially as applied to health care, but it is likely to be a preferable approach than traditional ABC.

Who's Counting

The idea of applying ABC disciplines to health care is not new. In fact, ABC was implemented in several European health systems many years ago.

In one particular case, the implementation focused on linking costs to diagnosis-related grouping (DRG) codes. Conceptually similar to the "grouper" approaches described in Chapter 7, the DRG system can allocate 12,000 different diagnoses into more than 500 illness groups. Group cost estimates include both fixed costs (e.g., inpatient stay, food, typical procedures) as well as variable costs (e.g., labs, scans). But as opposed to simply allocating money at the DRG level, ABC allows the organizations to see the real-world cost implications.

"In order to operate efficiently with charge control, it is absolutely imperative to establish an overview of the hospital's actual costs structures, and to create transparency and insight right across the organizations," explained one of the organizations' leaders.

In addition to providing information to support financial analyses, the system also enables individual organizations to benchmark their activities, set activity targets and measure attainment against those targets.

As we consider any costing methodology, it is important to acknowledge some aspects of health delivery and cost accrual that should influence our implementation:

- **Healthy Cost.** In our pursuit of health value, we may find that healthier patients might be more expensive within the epoch of time we are measuring: they live longer, may consume more preventative services, etc. So our costing approach should reflect this, and our conclusions from costing exercises have to be taken in this context.

- **Nonintegrated.** Health care today does not operate as a seamless, integrated collection of processes. The overall process being assessed is not just complicated; it crosses people, departments, institutions, markets, and time periods. Putting aside developing the actual costs, even assessing the business processes can be incredibly difficult when those processes do not fall under a common organizational governance model. It would be easy to develop costing models that assume integrated delivery, and those models would miss the potentially large costs associated with the nonintegrated design and execution of care delivery. The nonintegrated nature of the ecosystem may also limit the effectiveness and return on investment associated with the business improvements identified through cost analysis.

- **Time Interdependencies.** Recall from earlier chapters that "time" is a primary dimension of interest in assessing health, sometimes acting as a variable, an endpoint, and/or an assumption. It is also a primary interest area in costing methodologies like TDABC, where time's role can similarly vary. Any methodology that seeks to use time as a driver of costs must account for a complex set of interdependencies: the factors of time, health outcomes, and costs are not independent. The relationship can actually be recursive—time drives costs, which drive outcomes, which drive more time and costs which drive more outcomes (see Figure 8.3). Though it may be straightforward to measure time against activities and costs, the subsequent transition to value calculations is much more complicated.

- **Nonlinear.** Not only is health care not integrated, the execution of the processes are nonlinear as well. Though there is nothing inherently linear or sequential in methodologies such as TDABC, it is easy to fall into the mental trap of assuming incremental, as opposed to parallel and independent, cost accrual. This situation is especially true given the time interdependencies we just observed, as time is usually one of the biggest loss factors in measuring

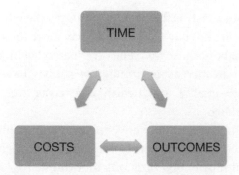

Figure 8.3 Time, Costs, and Outcomes are Interdependent.

processes spanning governance controls (i.e., business processes that operate across organizational lines can be less efficient than centralized processes due to the additional burdens of coordination, communication, process misalignment, and other issues).

- **Cost/Value Scope.** Any objective analysis of health care will eventually uncover a fundamental truth: health costs and value are unavoidably shared. Many of the things that make us human—empathy, ethics, justice, altruism, the pursuit of the common good and the reduction of suffering—mean that no matter how much we may want to think otherwise, health care will never be a product or service whose value is completely determined by individual consumer's experiences of that product or service. Value calculations that look perfectly reasonable from an individual consumer perspective will always be unavoidably connected to how we as a people manage our collective health risks and costs. Said another way, human morality carries a cost that is not in our equation (and it offers benefits as well).

None of these issues are showstoppers. They simply reflect design and implementation issues that we need to thoughtfully address in implementing TDABC or any other costing methodology. And in the end, the specific methodology of costing selected is likely less important than the overall imperative for pursuing a more detailed, accurate articulation of costs.

Linking Costs to Quality

In Western culture such as the United States, people tend to believe that cost and quality are directly related. If we pay more for a Mercedes than a Toyota, it must be because Mercedes are "better" vehicles. Yet over the past few years, an increasing number of studies have demonstrated that health care quality and health care costs are not necessarily positively correlated.

Whereas the association between cost and quality is certainly true in some consumer markets, some studies have shown the exact opposite in health care: organizations that can deliver a certain health service at a lower cost can produce superior results: better patient health outcomes, fewer quality and safety problems, etc. Why might this be true?

One hypothesis is that these organizations can charge less because they are better at delivering the service. If a hospital does four cardiac bypass surgeries every day, that organization has probably learned more about how to deliver that service safely and effectively than a hospital that does four bypass surgeries a month. Since efficiency and quality can translate into lower costs for the service provider, those cost savings can be passed on to consumers. And some data supports this hypothesis: service volume sometimes does correlate (inversely) with service cost.

Though time may prove this hypothesis to be true, we introduce this concept in a chapter on value because much of the work in analyzing these trends have been plagued by shortcomings that advanced analytics focused on value can help address:

- **Cost versus Price.** Any good economist can defend why cost and price are not always comparable, especially in asymmetrical markets. Though we usually have visibility to price, all too often we have little-to-no visibility to cost for the reasons discussed here. And since our hypothesis around pass-through cost benefits is contingent on knowing the cost basis for these services, initiatives such as activity-based costing and comparative analyses are needed before we can draw this conclusion.

- **Correlation versus Causation.** It is tempting to attribute causes where we see patterns, but the truth is often more difficult to uncover. We know there are many other variables that come into play in addition to service volume. For example, there are significant geographic differences in health risks, insurance coverage, reimbursement rates, and provider pay. Which of these factors has a more profound influence on cost? The careful and creative application of inferential statistics can help us move beyond the surface-level trends to really look at how costs vary.

Much to the dismay of those trying to develop consistent health policy recommendations, it is doubtful that the industry will find a single, simple, universal relationship between cost and service volume, quality, or outcomes . . . the factors involved are too complicated. But there are undoubtedly relationships between these factors, and those relationships can be properly characterized through advanced analytics.

LINKING COSTS TO RISK

One of the truly transformative opportunities in health care is the idea that, by combining the approaches we've covered in health outcomes analysis and costing models, we can actually begin to really associate health risks and costs.

Today, health risk and cost analyses are primarily retrospective, and limited in how richly both the risks and costs are defined. Most of the time, since we have historically lacked the tools and insights to characterize actual risk, health risk analyses have substituted actual disease manifestation for risk. The thinking goes something like this: if we look at how much a particular disease currently costs to treat, we can see a reasonably accurate indication of how much various health risks costs.

Though that hypothesis may be true, there are a lot of reasons to believe that it may also be flawed. First, a risk is usually something that has not happened yet; once the risk has happened, it is already incurring costs. Second, risk analyses are usually intended to support risk mitigation, yet retrospective views of disease manifestation offer no real insights into prevention (clinical or cost). Third, since our cost estimates have historically been based on a high level of cost granularity, we don't actually know how costs are accruing. And finally, and perhaps most importantly from an analytics perspective, disease may not be the most important dimension to predicting future health risks and costs. The manifestation of disease is certainly a valuable dimension to assess. But what if costs are more closely associated with other factors such as preferences, behaviors, geography, health program participation, diet, travel frequency, etc.? What if they are more closely determined by physician age, reimbursed health services, wellness incentives, care facility, the time on market for their prescription, etc.?

Chapter 11 is devoted to risk management. In terms of how risk management influences costs, our position is that health risk should be about more than medical history, weight, blood panels, and tobacco use. As our analytical capabilities grow to produce richer insights, our conceptualization of health risks and their associated costs will evolve as well.

VALUE INNOVATION

Kaplan and Porter's article on ABC was a great rallying point for an industry struggling to understand how to derive cost and value. What is the return on investment for understanding your own business? Can health care derive sufficient cost savings through process efficiencies to justify the expenditures in process reengineering derived from costing methodologies?

In the end, organizational appetites for detailed costing and value exercises may come down to simple risk avoidance. Today, providers cannot confidently enter into value-based contracting models because they can't fully articulate actual baseline costs. Payers cannot confidently enter value-based contracting because they lack visibility to the relationship between cost and value. And life sciences firms cannot make educated decisions about research and development (R&D) investments and corresponding pricing strategies because it is not clear what value a drug delivers—even drugs that have been on the market for twenty years! Everyone has a piece of the puzzle, but no one has all the pieces. These gaps in incorporating knowledge, incentives, and values into our overall decision-making frameworks erode the value derived from the entire system.

And yet, the opportunity for innovation is so large. Consider this: could a drug company develop a more cost effective treatment for a disease if they knew the actual costs of currently treating that disease? I strongly suspect the answer is yes. As pharmaceutical companies gradually acknowledge that their future business viability may be contingent on offering services in addition to products, there is a huge business opportunity in addressing cost and value issues. If a company's treatment will only be reimbursed based on comparative factors going forward, why limit the comparison to general product measures? The potential value, as we've defined it here, is much larger than that. And everyone wins.

NOTE

1. Examples include the *American Medical Association's Physician Consortium for Performance Improvement*® *Work Group on Efficiency and Cost of Care*. For a European perspective, see *The Health Foundation* report "Measuring Value for Money in Healthcare."

CHAPTER **9**

The New
Behavioral Health

DANGEROUS PORTALS

In November of 2012, the *Journal of the American Medical Association* published the "Association of Online Patient Access to Clinicians and Medical Records With Use of Clinical Services."[1] The research study involved an analysis of patients within the Kaiser health system, and compared those patients who used electronic tools such as Kaiser's patient portal with those patients who did not. The article's findings and conclusions set the blogosphere alive; one blog's headline read "The Electronic Health Record (EHR) Online Portal Increases Hospitalization Rates."

Putting aside the methodological, statistical, and interpretive aspects of the study (which are always subject to academic debate), why could it be true that a health system might see service utilization correlating with online activity? The first idea might be that these patients are sicker. But the study tried to control for that by creating a comparison group that was comparably sick, and the results still held true.

Another idea might be that online access to clinicians and information causes patients to consume more services. For example, it could be that allowing people to see their health information raises concerns that drive them to call their doctor or book more doctor appointments. And the study data actually supports this hypothesis—online users had more phone calls to their physicians, for example. But the study did not explore the root causes of that increased activity—were the questions about their medical records, or were the patients who were using the online system using it because they were orchestrating care with their physician? These patients also had more hospital admissions, which may or may not be discretionary. So since correlation does not equal causation, the study actually doesn't address this hypothesis.

But there are some other ideas that may hold the keys to understanding this phenomenon, and they derive from the science of psychology.

THE HEALTH-MINDEDNESS GENE EXPERIMENT

Let's do a thought experiment. Suppose for a moment that there is a "health-mindedness" gene. The gene is expressed in individuals who are predisposed to more involvement, activity, and commitment to their own health: they regularly visit their doctor, ask their doctor questions, read about their medical conditions online, and take all of their medicine on time. They think about health issues, and make decisions based in part on their understanding of health.

Consider three questions about these health-mindedness patients:

1. Would these people consume more health services? Possibly— they would be more likely to discuss health issues with their providers, engage in preventative medicine, and behave proactively in seeking solutions when issues arise.

2. Would they have superior health outcomes? Hopefully preventative medicine, health risk awareness, education, and early intervention should in theory produce improved outcomes.

3. Are these patients more cost effective overall? We have no idea, but we like to think so because they would likely be "smarter consumers" of health (i.e., as opposed to going to the hospital for seasonal allergies).

So, we could easily theorize that our fictional health-mindedness gene—as an inherent aspect of an individual—could determine both health outcomes and costs. We can't say exactly how it would impact outcomes and costs—that would need to be a topic of empirical research— but it seems reasonable to hypothesize that there would be a relationship.

Now, if you can imagine this possibility, then consider there are a huge number of nonfictional, real-world personal factors that could have the same sort of deterministic effect on outcomes and costs.

ENGEL'S MODEL

What if some of the things that make people unique—their skills, personalities, belief systems, socioeconomic conditions, etc.—actually determine, at least in part, their health outcomes and costs?

In 1977, a psychiatrist named George L. Engel at the University of Rochester published a paper[2] in the prestigious journal *Science*. In it, he posited that health and illness are actually the products of a complex interplay between biological, psychological, and social factors. This idea was fairly revolutionary, and reflected a gradual movement across all of the sciences away from a reductionistic view of the universe (such as simple cause-and-effect relationships) towards a more systems-oriented view. Today, we take for granted that there are no easy answers to a lot of science's questions, but this idea was not widely shared in medicine at that time. Engel proposed that both researchers and practitioners develop a more holistic approach to understanding and treating patients; his idea was termed the "biopsychosocial model."

If you've never heard of the biopsychosocial model, you are not alone. The idea was transformative in its conceptualization of medicine, but it has not been widely adopted in practice[3] due at least in part to the difficulty in procedurally implementing such an approach. However, modern concepts around "patient-centeredness" evolved from the ideas reflected in Engel's model.[4]

It would not be difficult to theorize that patients' characteristics influence their experience of the health delivery system:

- Are patients who are more active or comfortable in social situations more likely to get information (and the right information) from their physicians? Does assertiveness influence patients' health outcomes?

- Do patients who are more "action-oriented" consume more health services (i.e., because they are more likely do something when facing a choice) or less health services (i.e., because they are more likely to engage in preventative activities)? Is this what creates "engaged patients"?

- Do patients who regularly participate in a spiritual tradition consume health differently? Does the tradition matter?

- Do patients who worry a lot consume health services in greater volumes? How does a patient's anxiety change the climate of care delivery that they receive?

- Are patients who are more prone to decreased affective responses (e.g., depression) less likely to consume health services when needed, ultimately increasing their health expenditures due to escalation and lack of prevention?

Research already exists that explore many of these questions. For example, Dr. D. J. Cegala at The Ohio State University has shown that physicians' interactions with their patients differ based on patient social traits: prognosis, treatment options, surgical procedures, treatment benefits, risks, side effects, and even overall patient-centeredness all varied based on patient traits. In fact, the overwhelming majority of medical and psychological research today shows that Engel's idea—if not the actual model—was absolutely right: health outcomes (and therefore costs) are dramatically influenced by a confluence of these factors in addition to the underlying biological mechanisms.

So it is not really a question of whether many of these factors influence health outcomes and costs. The questions are more complex now: what factors, how, when, for whom exactly, how much, how strongly predictive, etc. And these questions are health analytics questions.

THE NEW EVOLVING SCIENCE OF BEHAVIORAL HEALTH

If health outcomes and costs are not just a result of the disease or the patient's genetic makeup, how do we begin to understand the forces that are at play?

Health analytics are a young discipline in being able to characterize this incredibly complex landscape. But it is probably reasonable to assume that the problem space consists of at least four dimensions:

1. **What You Are**—the biological traits, characteristics, predispositions, and propensities that characterize an individual.

2. **What You Experience**—the collection of life events and their corresponding impacts on an individual.

3. **What You Do**—the activities, actions, and impacts that an individual makes and experiences.

4. **What You Believe**—the mental, emotional, and spiritual framework through which an individual sees and experiences the world. This vector obviously includes religious beliefs, but also includes values and cultural norms.

The goal of health analytics in this context, then, is to help characterize these four dimensions: What are the factors within each dimension? How does each factor contribute to an individual's health outcomes/costs? and How do the dimensions and factors interact?

CASE STUDY

Behavioral Health

The term "behavioral health" is routinely used to describe many different aspects of the intersections between psychology and medicine. Though it is used here to describe a growing discipline of personalized care interactions, it is important to highlight that other implications of the term "behavioral health"—such as mental health, for example—are equally important.

In one notable case, researchers uncovered through an analysis of regional health data sources that, over a five-year period, ten percent of physician visits and ten percent of hospitalizations were due to mental health issues. From the perspective of health outcomes and costs, such a situation creates many undesirable effects, including:

- Suboptimal care delivery by organizations and staff inadequately equipped to deal with mental health disorders
- Unnecessary exposure of patients to infectious diseases, medical errors, and other risks
- Improper use of high-cost health services

It is likely that, especially within urban centers, mental health represents a much higher proportion of health services utilization. Analytics can be used not only to measure and model these trends, but also to test the effectiveness of various interventions designed to improve outcomes and costs: early detection and intervention initiatives, training programs, community outreach, provider collaboration, and alternative patient triage processes.

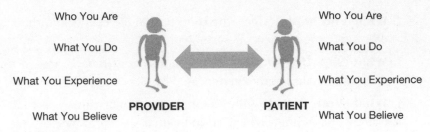

Figure 9.1 Individual Dimensions.

Before we go on, though, we need to acknowledge an important point. In addition to patients, health care delivery involves another set of human beings with their own sets of predispositions and personalities. It is not just patients' profiles along these four dimensions that determine health outcomes and costs—it is also their providers (see Figure 9.1).

For too long, our analyses of provider behaviors have been focused on cost and activity analysis: who orders the most procedures, prescribes which medications, has faster patient throughput, etc. But research[5] has shown more than twenty physician factors that seem to influence patient health outcomes: empathy, dominant vs. passive physician styles, humor, physician education, friendliness, courtesy, many aspects of body language, and a wide variety of verbal behaviors.

So trying to assess the four dimensions—who you are, what you experience, what you do, and what you believe—purely from the patient's perspective is somewhat akin to trying to characterize the behavior of water molecules by studying oxygen atoms. It is only in combination with hydrogen that the emergent properties of water are actually observable. Likewise, until we can more reliably discern the relative weight of each patient and physician factor, we must assume that we need to study both.

WHAT YOU ARE

The genetic sciences are absolutely transforming our understanding of human biology. Individuals carry in their cells both explanations for existing conditions as well as warning signs of potential future problems. As our understanding of the human genome continues its rapid pace of development, more and more patient biological information will become available to medical practitioners to aid the diagnosis and treatment of disease. The size, volume, and complexity of the data and analytics involved in understanding the human genome and its expression will be an ongoing opportunity for health analytics for the next century.

But people are more than their genomic profile; they have minds and personalities. Entire fields of psychology are dedicated to the study of individual personality, and have generated numerous instruments and taxonomies that describe varying aspects of individuals and their predispositions. How do these individual factors influence health care? Would we expect to see variations in both patients and physicians based on dimensions such as personality traits, learning styles, intelligence, developmental differences, and gender? Table 9.1 summarizes traits that have emerged through psychology that may prove instructive.

Table 9.1 Sample Traits

Sample Personality Traits	Cattell's Personality Factors
▪ Agreeableness	▪ Abstractedness
▪ Alexithymia	▪ Apprehension
▪ Conscientiousness	▪ Dominance
▪ Disinhibition	▪ Emotional Stability
▪ Extraversion	▪ Liveliness
▪ Harm avoidance	▪ Openness to Change
▪ Impulsivity	▪ Perfectionism
▪ Neuroticism	▪ Privateness
▪ Novelty seeking	▪ Reasoning
▪ Obsessionality	▪ Rule-Consciousness
▪ Openness to experience	▪ Self-Reliance
▪ Perfectionism	▪ Sensitivity
▪ Psychoticism	▪ Social Boldness
▪ Rigidity	▪ Tension
▪ Self-Esteem	▪ Vigilance
	▪ Warmth
Minnesota Multiphasic Personality Inventory (sample)	**Myers-Briggs Type Indicator**
▪ Hypochondriasis	▪ Attitudes: Extraversion versus Introversion
▪ Depression	▪ Perceiving Function: Sensing versus Intuition
▪ Hysteria	▪ Judging Function: Thinking versus Feeling

(continued)

Table 9.1 (*Continued*)

Minnesota Multiphasic Personality Inventory (sample)	Myers-Briggs Type Indicator
■ Masculinity/Femininity ■ Psychasthenia ■ Social Introversion ■ Lie Propensity ■ Defensiveness ■ Response Inconsistency ■ Superlative Self-Presentation ■ Ego Strength ■ Dominance ■ Addictions Potential ■ Social Discomfort ■ Anxiety ■ Repression ■ Type A	■ Lifestyle: Judging versus Perception

Today, we lack consensus within the medical community on the mechanisms we should use to define, measure, and analyze these factors in both patients and providers. But we have a rich history of psychological research to draw from as we undertake our investigations.

WHAT YOU EXPERIENCE

No matter what genetic and personal attributes individuals carry, everyone is also a product of his or her own experiences. Even the expression of our genomic propensities is mediated by exposure to environmental factors.

Our life experiences "load" individuals with both capabilities and shortcomings. An only child experiences the world differently than the fourth of six children. Individuals completing formal education have a different set of attributes than those lacking in formal education. Soldiers that have been through the trauma of war carry physical, mental, and emotional scars and conditions that are more prevalent than in the nonmilitary population. Workers who are exposed to toxic or carcinogenic substances carry a different risk profile than a banker. Individuals from poor communities are different than individuals from more affluent communities.

Let's consider just one aspect of what we experience: geography. At a TEDMED medical technology and health care event in 2009, Bill Davenhall gave a talk entitled "Your Health Depends on Where You Live." By combining geo-spatial and health data, Bill was able to show how health risks actually materialize differently across the various geographies and states within the United States. What could account for these geographic variations? Pollution, diet, manufacturing by-products, industrial accidents, sun exposure, hobbies . . . the list goes on. His point was that a person's lifetime geographic experience—the places you have lived and worked—should be a part of everyone's medical record. I suspect he is right.

WHAT YOU DO

Your doctor has probably asked you the questions during your checkup: do you eat healthy? Do you smoke, drink, and/or use illegal drugs? Do you exercise? The activities, actions, and decisions we make have a huge—some might even argue deterministic—impact on our health.

There is no question that healthier lifestyle decisions produce improved health—you don't need a lot of health analytics to figure that out. The real health analytics opportunity resides in the tremendous amount of supplemental data that exists about what you do. Do you use a grocery store loyalty card? Your purchase history says a lot about your risk factors. How much money do you make? Your income level likely drives how frequently you dine out, and whether you can afford fresh vegetables.

An entire data industry has erupted over the past decade. There are multiple firms in the United States that aggregate literally thousands of variables about individual consumers—credit profiles, magazine subscriptions, interests, travel, Web sites, purchase histories, TV viewing patterns—that can be used to develop all sorts of health innovations: novel approaches to health risk assessments, improvements in disease management programs, better targeting for medical outreach, etc. Though many U.S. consumers feel somewhat uneasy with the idea that their data is being collected, the reality is that the horse has left the gate.

One of the more interesting aspects of what you do is reflected in social media activity. Many consumer-facing organizations such as retail and consumer goods firms have looked to social media for understanding commercial issues such as brand sentiment and customer support, and health care is following that path as well. But we also see more clinical applications in the social information that individuals readily provide on a daily basis. In the example of the National Collaborative for Bio-Preparedness (NCB-Prepared) we discussed in Chapter 7, data mining of consumer social media and other data could assist in predicting the epidemiological spread of communicable diseases weeks before the actual spread of the disease. And it would not be difficult to imagine that Twitter users who tweet about their participation in a major marathon are likely at decreased risk of cardiovascular disease, but potentially greater risk for hip and knee replacement.

But you don't have to be into social media data to see immediate opportunities in new uses of individual data in the service of health improvements. Consider for a moment that, as an employer, your company likely has a lot of information about you that could aid in predicting and managing your health:

- Health and wellness program participation (fitness, disease management, weight loss, integrative medicine)
- Absentee history (sick leave, vacation utilization, family medical leave)
- Workers compensation, disability, and ergonomics data
- Environmental exposure (e.g., risk factors)
- Insurance coverage (e.g., available vs. consumed health care services)
- Meal content (e.g., onsite cafeterias, onsite storefronts)
- Time on premises (e.g., badge reader data, work/life balance)
- Expense report items (e.g., restaurant and bar utilization, travel and geography history)
- Credit reports (e.g., employment screening)
- Performance evaluations (e.g., work quality, job satisfaction)

As employers continue to explore how to simultaneously reduce health costs while differentiating themselves in a more competitive health insurance market, it is likely we will see employers taking a more active role in health management. And many other companies are pursuing these nascent big data opportunities as well. What you do will become much more important in health care.

WHAT YOU BELIEVE

Anyone who is familiar with the placebo effect has seen the impact that beliefs can have on an individual's experience of health. In short, a patient can experience a clinical benefit from a treatment regardless of the treatment's clinical efficacy based solely on whether the patient believes the treatment will be effective. The lens through which a patient views the world can have a fundamental impact on the outcomes they experience.

Another example is spirituality. Religion and spiritual beliefs and practices among patients have been positively associated with a huge range of health benefits: life expectancy; better immune function; improvements in heart disease and blood pressure; lower cholesterol; and better health behaviors.[6] We also know that some religious beliefs impact medical decision-making, conflict with medical care, and can produce stress and impair health outcomes. In short, our beliefs have a huge impact on how we operate in the world around us.

As health care becomes less local and more regional, national, and international, cultural expectations and norms—often difficult to quantify or even define concretely—are similarly important in growing our understanding of health. Culture pervades almost every aspect of our experience of health care: what we think, how we act, the ways we communicate, the actions we take, and the decisions we make are all mediated by our views of the world around us. And all of these things can potentially impact health outcomes and costs.

INFLUENCING CHANGE

So far, our discussion of the four questions—what you are, what you experience, what you do, and what you believe—has focused on identifying these factors. But the real challenge is behavior *change*: once you know there is a relationship, how can you influence a more positive outcome from patients and/or physicians?

Behavioral change—particularly sustained behavioral change—is hard. It is also required. And much of our understanding around how to produce sustainable change is still rather immature. Whether it is getting patients to exercise or getting providers to wash their hands, our efforts to date have usually been "brute force": we just keep telling people what they need to do until they do it. And that approach has not really worked.

One of the reasons some people believe we have not been successful in producing meaningful change is because we lack visibility and understanding of the individual factors covered in this chapter. In short, you cannot improve what you do not measure.

Another reason, though, is that our behavioral interventions rarely address more than one or two of the four questions. A physician hand-washing campaign implemented through signs all over the ward is really only trying to impact "what you do." But we know any individual's behavior is a reflection of all of their unique attributes. For some people, signs might work. For others, increased education and data about the relationship between hand washing and avoidable medical complications (i.e., what you experience) will be critical. For others, linking hand washing to an empathetic, altruistic message on protecting patients (what you believe) may be the most motivational thing to do.

In this context, health care needs to accept a fundamental truth: the responsibility for ensuring a communication is effective resides with the message sender, not the message receiver. If we want to influence behavioral change, our interventions should be designed to meet our target audience—patients, providers, even industry executives—on their own terms.

PUTTING INTO PRACTICE

In this chapter, we've proposed a lot of different issues that should be the subject of medical and translational research. Some will prove to be instrumental in improving health outcomes and costs; others will not. And some new game changers not covered here will undoubtedly emerge as well. As discussed earlier, the innovation opportunity is only limited by creativity. But it begins by acknowledging that dimensions that are health relevant to individuals include a much wider variety than what is in their medical charts today.

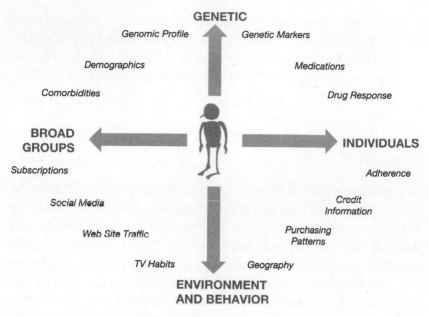

Figure 9.2 Dimensions of Health-Relevant Data.

Two questions, though, face every health organization:

1. How do we create and/or collect individual-level data like this? You have three choices: collect, buy, and/or derive. You can start collecting the information within the processes and assets that you already use to collect patient and provider information. You can also look to purchase data from third-party aggregators. And finally, in the absence of collected or purchased data, you can use data that you already have to derive some surrogate markers— data points that might not be as good as the real data, but could serve to start the exploration. My recommendation is to do all three, as they all have strengths and weaknesses.

2. How can you compare and contrast research and findings across multiple organizations when they will undoubtedly have different data sources, methods, and even conceptualizations of a meaningful factor? This issue is harder, in that we do not have—and likely will not have in the foreseeable future—data taxonomies supported by industry consensus. But remember, that is the nature of science. The first ones exploring the unknown take a stab at a

framework for understanding things, and over time others join in, refine, discard, and reengineer until we generally agree. In the age of health analytics, we at least enjoy the benefits of an accelerated process through the use of information technology.

The evolution of a new discipline like behavioral health is never easy. But we can get there.

OUTCOMES

Returning to the George Engel article in *Science* discussed at the beginning of this chapter, it is interesting to note that the study does not look at health outcomes. In this book, we build the case for health analytics as a discipline that—by necessity—links clinical, financial/operational, and individual data together. In focusing on only operational dimensions (e.g., frequency of online access to information, physician interactions), we are not able to draw any real conclusions about how to guide health transformation. Maybe medical record access does increase utilization. Or maybe it doesn't. Maybe an increase in this type of utilization escalates costs, or maybe it doesn't. Maybe patients are healthier because they are behaviorally engaged in their care through this online technology, or maybe not. Without analytics that link clinical and individual dimensions to behaviors, we are just wandering around Chapter 1's Alexandrian library hoping we stumble on the right book.

■ Getting Personal

CASE STUDY

If you think getting to individual behavioral decision-making is just too far out of reach, consider the case of a European health institute. Faced with rising costs in chronic condition management, the institute developed an analytical solution that enables both providers and patients to make more personalized decisions about care.

Patients use the solution to specify their health priorities, lifestyle factors, and up to four factors (e.g., sleep, diet, exercise) that they would be willing to improve. The analytical solution then provides a systematic test plan that, when executed and compiled, allows the patient to see which combination of factors had the most beneficial results based on their personal priorities. The solution actually analyzes every combination of factors to find the optimal solution for the individual patient.

Supporting this work, the organization also collects patient- and provider-generated encounter information to assist physicians in making care decisions. By analyzing over 150,000 consultations covering more than 20,000 patients, physicians can predict the results of administering various combinations of drug therapies for the individual patient.

"[Clinical] guidelines were drawn up based on clinical trials with 'normal patients' and do not always suit the individual patient at an ordinary clinic," said one of the directors of the organization.

NOTES

1. Palen, T. E., Ross, C., Powers, J. D., and Xu, S. (2012). "Association of Online Patient Access to Clinicians and Medical Records With Use of Clinical Services." *Journal of the American Medical Association*. 308(19): 2012–2019.

2. Engel, G. (April 8, 1977). "The Need for a New Medical Model: a Challenge for Biomedicine." *Science* 196 (4286): 129–136.

3. For example, see Alonso, Y. (2004). "The Biopsychosocial Model in Medical Research: the Evolution of the Health Concept Over the Last Two Decades." *Patient Educational Counseling.* May; 53(2): 239–44.

4. Smith, R. (2002). "The Biopsychosocial Revolution: Interviewing and Provider-Patient Relationships Becoming Key Issues for Primary Care." *Journal of General Internal Medicine,* 17(4): 309–310.

5. Beck, R.S., Daughtridge, R., and Sloane, P.D. (2002). "Physician-Patient Communication in the Primary Care Office: A Systematic Review." *Journal of the American Board of Family Practice.* 15(1): 25–38.

6. Koenig, H. (2004). "Religion, Spirituality, and Medicine: Research Findings and Implications for Clinical Practice." *Southern Medical Journal.*

CHAPTER 10

Customer Insights

THE CONSUMERIZED PATIENT

It is now clear: health care in the future will be more consumer-directed. Consumers will have a greater say in where they receive health services, what insurance they carry, and how their health care dollars are spent. They will pick care providers who offer the best experience. They will select insurance based more closely on their individual needs. They will use services that deliver more value than pills. They will be more informed; they will care about quality and costs, and they will carry more responsibility and accountability for their own health.

Accordingly, organizations across the health ecosystem—providers, payers, pharmaceutical product manufacturers, and others—need to care more about what customers are saying, how they are experiencing products and services, and how this information should be informing their business plans and strategies. Health care is gradually growing up to be more like other consumer markets. So the question facing every health organization is simple: how are you gaining the insights needed to be successful and profitable in this individualized market?

WILL THE REAL CUSTOMER PLEASE STAND UP?

I was recently in a meeting with the sales and marketing leadership team for a large pharmaceutical company. During the meeting, the word "customer" was being used a lot in the context of the firm's future commercial strategy. One of the newer employees in the room finally asked the obvious question: "When we are saying customer, can someone just clarify for me who we are talking about?" For a good portion of the next 30 minutes, we tried (arguably without much success) to answer that question.

In the evolving ecosystem called health care, there are a lot of "customers." And by that, we don't mean a large number of individuals, though that is true as well. We are talking about a large number of types of customers. The answer to "who is the customer?" is not just dependent on the organization you are talking to; it depends on to whom in the organization you might be speaking. Candidates for the title of customer can include (among others):

- Patients
- Physicians
- Payers
- Regulators
- Suppliers
- Employers
- Researchers
- Government
- Retailers

Notice anything interesting about this list? Yes; it is the same list that we define as the health ecosystem. If you are in the health ecosystem, at some point everyone else in the ecosystem is your customer.

If that seems like an overgeneralization, consider the pharmaceutical company above. No one would argue that patients are customers since they consume and benefit from the product. But historically, physicians have been considered a main customer since they make the product decisions when they write the prescriptions. Except nowadays, no matter what prescription they write, the payer may determine what is actually purchased. Those policies, preferences, and decisions can change periodically, though, based on incentives offered by wholesale suppliers and retailers. And the drug will never get to market unless evidence from researchers convinces government regulators to approve it.

No matter where you look, there are now multiple constituents that maintain a perception of your brand and contribute to your profitability. Providers have to care about recruiting physicians and patients, satisfying payer contracting terms, creating preferred vendor relationships with local employers, and satisfying regulatory reporting around clinical, financial, and administrative information. The diversification of "customers" is endemic across the health ecosystem.

To date, health and life sciences organizations have not widely used "customer intelligence" analytics as broadly as other industries. There are several reasons for this, including:

- **Lack of Commercial Analytical Competencies.** Many organizations have had little to no experience in using any marketing-related analytics other than basic Web traffic. Those organizations that do have experience have usually been focused on descriptive statistics, such as Web site traffic, grouping physician sales leads based on prescription volume, and call center metrics. In many cases, firms have outsourced any analytics-related work to firms specializing in analytical talent, avoiding the need to staff the expertise in house.

- **Lack of Transparency.** To do commercial analytics well, you need to bring lots of diverse data together. When organizations have failed to collect, license, or partner for the data that fuels their insights, it has been difficult to envision how advanced analytics could help.

- **Privacy Concerns.** There are both real and perceived constraints on the use of commercially relevant data. More importantly, the regulatory and legal concerns over health data have created corporate cultures where innovation is inhibited. Even where the use of data is both warranted and permissible, all too often the answer is "We can't do that sort of thing."

- **Lack of a Clear Mandate to Do So.** Prior to U.S. health reform, many organizations lacked incentives for developing stronger commercial competencies. If a health plan is not selling directly to consumers, there isn't much need for consumer-level analytics. As long as pharmaceutical companies could maintain a reasonable level of profitability using broad-based physician targeting, the motivation for optimizing that profitability was diminished.

But these issues are changing. During periods of rapid change, long-term business viability is no longer assured. In the face of escalating costs and business model challenges, all of the various customers in the health ecosystem are getting smarter and more informed. In the future, successful health and life sciences organizations will be those that have mastered aggregating customer data and are making business decisions based on that data. And the successful leader will be one that establishes both the clear organizational mandate to become more customer-centric, and dismantles the competency and cultural barriers preventing true customer-centricity from emerging.

For those leaders, there is good news: other industries have already learned how to use analytics to drive sales and marketing more efficiently and effectively, and their knowledge is directly transferrable to health care. A global bank uses analytics to target cross-selling of financial products. A national retailer uses analytics to increase the response rate of customer emails. A national cell phone service reduces customer turnover by predicting which customers are likely to leave, and proactively engages to retain them. An online photo service increases revenue forecasting by better predicting advertising responses. An entertainment company increases profitability by targeting marketing campaigns to their most profitable customers. Most other industries have been using customer analytics for a while, and the value is clear.

WHAT ARE CUSTOMER ANALYTICS?

As a domain of advanced analytics, customer analytics, or "customer intelligence" is an incredibly broad and diverse set of business insights covering many aspects of an organization: marketing, sales, business development, and customer support are just a few of the many functions that need customer insights. And though we use the term "commercial" fairly frequently, we are not implying any particular business model or entity structure. By definition, every organization has at least one customer (otherwise, there would be no need for the organization). So every organization—for-profit or nonprofit, public or private, academic or commercial, public or private sector—needs customer insights.

Due to the diversity of organizational functions that require customer insights, it can be difficult to nail down a single set of objectives that customer insights are intended to address. Common areas of focus include:

- Growing a customer base
- Ensuring optimal expense allocation
- Improving profitability
- Improving the performance of programs and assets such as marketing campaigns
- Increasing customer satisfaction and experience
- Improving corporate brand identity

Note that in the health ecosystem, each of these objectives can have multiple "faces" to them—clinical, financial, or administrative. For example, the goal of improving the performance of programs could be applied in terms of the administrative execution of marketing programs. It could also be deployed as improving disease management programs and their associated clinical outcomes. Table 10.1 provides some examples of how customer intelligence can be applied.

A FRAMEWORK OF CUSTOMER ANALYTICS

The framework we use for undertaking customer analytics is fairly consistent. It is a process whereby we:

- Bring together what is known about the customers;
- Develop some predictive models for what happens in the real world;
- Look for groupings of those customers ("customer segments") that reliably predict some clinical, financial, and/or commercial concerns;

Table 10.1 Examples of Customer Intelligence

	Clinical	Financial	Administrative
Growing Customers	▪ Targeting untapped patient communities	▪ Identifying the most profitable customers	▪ Automating customer acquisition
Expense Allocation	▪ Aligning marketing to clinical populations	▪ Aligning sales resources	▪ Aligning marketing expenses to channels
Increased Profitability	▪ Guiding patients to services based on risk	▪ Increased revenue forecasting accuracy	▪ Social network and sentiment analysis
Program Performance	▪ Improving disease management	▪ Campaign management	▪ Customer churn analysis
Customer Experience	▪ Improving adherence	▪ Growing therapeutic reputation	▪ Communication channel optimization

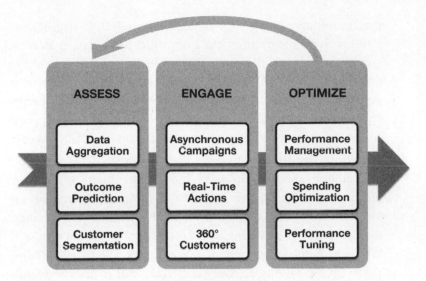

Figure 10.1 Three Phases of Customer Analytics.

- Implement some form of engagement, improvement, or business process focused on achieving some business objective with those customer segments;
- Measure what happens and refine our segments and models accordingly.

There are, of course, many variations to this theme, but this approach—representing phases of assessment, engagement, and optimization—reasonably captures a good portion of customer analytics scenarios (see Figure 10.1).

Let's look at each of these phases briefly.

Assess

The Assess phase is where the organization is planning what and how customer analytics will be used to improve the business.

- **Data Aggregation.** Arguably the most time consuming part of customer analytics, data aggregation is not just about collecting your own data about your customers (though in many cases that represents a rather large challenge as well). Data aggregation also involves integrating data from third-party data providers, and depending on the analytical problem you are looking to address, it is possible that third-party data may be superior to your own. Regardless, the many issues we discussed in earlier chapters on analytics and data—sample sizes, data quality, data completeness—are all factors that are considered in this work.

- **Outcome Prediction.** In the end, we want to develop predictive models about customers. The exact dimensions we are seeking to predict depends on the problem space we are working in: an individual's likelihood to respond to a marketing message, their propensity to participate in a disease management program, Web site behavior, a patient's health risk, even profitability. These predictive models will start crude, but over time will be refined and tuned based on real-world experience.

- **Customer Segmentation.** What constitutes a meaningful group of customers? If we are looking at a pool of 10,000 patients, for example, you might think that a disease or condition might be a useful way of grouping customers together for clinical interventions (i.e., engage all of the patients with diabetes). If

Group Dynamics

CASE STUDY

For organizations investing in more advanced capabilities for customer analytics, customer segmentation and outcome prediction are often a place where early value is derived. Examples of success are becoming increasingly available, such as:

- One global insurer used data mining and predictive modeling to determine customer segments that provided both the best promotional response as well as the greatest probability of policy persistence.
- A disease management company developed customer segments based on predicting clinical risks, the probability of experiencing care gaps, and the likelihood of interventional program success.
- A national blood bank used customer segmentation analytics to identify which individuals among 500,000 active donors are most likely to respond to promotional campaigns.

you are looking at a marketing campaign, zip codes may be a segmentation approach. Almost invariably, an organization starts the customer analytics process with a preconceived notion of what the customer segmentation should be. And though it is easy to guess how customers should be segmented, in customer analytics, it is often best to let the data tell you what the most meaningful segmentation approach might be. In all likelihood, analytics can detect a segmentation approach that is multivariate; in other words, more than one variable might combine to produce better segments that will improve results.

Engage

The Engage phase is where the organization is actually interacting with customers.

- **Asynchronous Campaigns.** Marketing campaigns are designed to drive new business, and the number of channels we use for those campaigns is growing: print, TV, radio, direct mail, telemarketing, email, mobile, and more. Campaign management is more than sending marketing messages. Any repeatable process of timely communication with a customer can be a campaign. A disease management program, for example, is a great example of a campaign. Marketing analytics software can automate the execution of campaigns as well as measure performance of the various messages, channels, and customer segments.

- **Real-Time Actions.** Ideally, we want more than our message delivered. Increasingly, organizations are looking to guide customers in real-time. For example, a health plan might want to proactively guide a potential customer to a particular insurance plan, or steer an existing customer towards a disease management program. Real-time analytics can be based on analytical models, or simply respond to triggering events such as a customer indicating an interest area. In either case, analytics actually helps customers get the most applicable information, products, and services for their particular needs.

- **360° Customers.** An individual customer interacts with your organization in many different ways. A physician conducting a clinical trial for a pharmaceutical company may also be receiving marketing literature related to the company's other products, speaking with the company's sales executives, contacting the call center with product safety questions, and speaking at a company-sponsored conference. To manage relationships effectively, organizations need 360° visibility to all of the various points of contact. Not only does such visibility increase effective communications and interactions, it also helps mitigate risks (e.g., exceeding physician payment limits).

Optimize

The Optimize phase is where all of the information from the prior phases comes together to improve future business.

- **Performance Management.** Throughout the Engage phase, organizations need the ability to monitor in real time how their marketing efforts are performing. Which messages are working? Which customer segments are not responding? Which channels are more effective? These and many other observable issues and measures are used to help drive optimization.

- **Spending Optimization.** Once we have performance information, it is important to ask the question "How can we get more for our marketing dollars?" Historically, organizations have often used descriptive statistics to make funding allocation decisions— whichever things appear to work best get more money. But there are many factors that should determine where, how, and how much marketing investments are made, and in advanced analytical terms, that is an optimization problem.

- **Performance Tuning.** Based on experience, we can always improve. Markets and customers are not static, and all of the above—customer segments, campaigns, profitability, etc. —move through time. Moving beyond descriptive statistics into predictive modeling enables organizations to optimize results, and tuning allows us to recursively learn and respond to the real

Reducing House Calls

Historically, pharmaceutical sales organizations segmented their targeted physicians into deciles based on prescription volume—the more prescriptions a physician wrote within a particular drug category, the more likely that physician would end up on a call list by pharmaceutical sales staff. A whole industry has emerged that provides outsourced services to pharmaceutical firms related to this approach.

Though relatively easy to implement, deciles ignore the fact that individual physicians differ in how they develop confidence and experience in new drug therapies. An individual physician may show preferences towards product samples, personalized medical education, industry conferences, self-directed learning, vouchers, and scientific literature among others. So a lot of wasted time, effort, and money can be spent targeting the wrong physicians with the wrong information.

One of the top ten pharmaceutical companies decided to try a different approach by developing a more sophisticated propensity-scoring model. These models were fed by a wide variety of physician and consumer data, including prior prescription transactions, geography, census, demographics, product sample distribution, promotional response, and call center data.

By identifying physician preferences and tendencies, the company achieved a nearly 50% reduction in physician face-to-face sales calls. They also saw a reduction in required sales staff to achieve the same sales coverage, and a doubling of the sales support capacity with no additional headcount. And because the work was in-house, they saved an additional $4MM in outsourcing. As final proof of the value of customer analytics, geographic targets that emerged from the analyses demonstrated a 75% sales growth rate as compared to the more typical 15%.

world. And as opposed to tuning decisions once a year, advanced analytics can empower organizations to make adjustments as frequently as needed.

SHARING INSIGHTS

Organizations can gain tremendous insight in developing customer analytics with their own data (whether in-house or licensed from a third party). And in many cases, the insights derived will be competitively sensitive. But not all of the insights should be treated as completely private because even greater business returns can be created through collaboration. Let's look at a specific example to illustrate this point.

Let's assume for a moment that a health plan undertakes a customer segmentation and campaign program around disease management. Because we are using advanced analytics throughout that program, the health plan will learn a lot more about the target population of patients than whether the program worked or not. They will have insight into which customer segmentation models were most predictive; in other words, they will learn about what factors are important in characterizing patients with this disease.

If providers had access to these insights, could they be more effective in prevention and intervention with patients? It is hard to say, but it is certainly reasonable to think that providers would be able to use that information to improve their own patient programs, especially if they connected this information to their own data repositories about their patient populations. Would such provider-initiated work help reduce health expenditures for the health plan? Potentially yes, especially if a significant portion of the provider's patients were covered by this plan. Would the health plan's original disease management program have been more effective if the health plan had partnered with the provider to develop the program by sharing data? Absolutely.

Now let's take that one step further. Could the pharmaceutical company that makes the most commonly prescribed drug for this disease use the program data to further research? Most likely yes, as the program will have collected a lot of information that the pharmaceutical company would not have studied. Would it make sense for the pharmaceutical company to join in a provider-payer partnership? It would seem to be in everyone's interest, as the combined data and knowledge would likely have a much more significant impact on disease prevention and management than any single organization could have hoped for on their own. Health outcomes improve. Costs are decreased. Organizational brands improve. Patients are healthier, happier, and more productive.

ADHERENCE

If this idea of shared insights seems too "pie in the sky," maybe it is. But consider for a moment the problem of adherence. Medication adherence, sometimes referred to as patient compliance, refers to the degree to which patients fill and take their prescriptions. There is a surprising amount of data to suggest that adherence is a source of many health issues. Nonadherent patients experience more health issues because their conditions are not being properly managed. Pharmaceutical companies and retailers lose money—by some industry estimates, billions of dollars—because customers are not filling their prescriptions. And providers are unable to make good care decisions because they can't always be certain that the treatments prescribed are actually being followed.

Why aren't patients compliant with their medications? This problem has been studied for a while, and a variety of reasons are often cited:

- **Cost**—patients may not be able to afford the treatments, or even the co-pays.
- **Undesirable Effects**—patients experience adverse events or side effects from the treatments, and are therefore discouraged from taking them.
- **Confidence**—patients don't believe the treatments are effective or necessary.
- **Logistics**—patients may struggle to get to the pharmacy due to work, lack of transportation, etc.

The truth resides in some combination of these factors (plus some things we probably don't yet know). Customer analytics can give us the tools to assess all of these factors, and importantly, determine which are most important for this patient, this disease, this geography, this care facility, this physician, this insurer, this insurance plan, and this pharmacy.

We invariably start these analytical exercises by trying to gain better insights into "what" is happening, but our end goals of understanding "why" and "how" require us to at least assess how individual differences contribute to what we observe. As you can probably tell by now, the personal attributes we discussed in our behavioral health chapter as contributing to health outcomes and costs are very important in customer analytics. The behavior of individuals—and our ability to predict that behavior—is usually one of the most important dimensions we are seeking to understand.

If disease management programs have failed to produce meaningful improvements in costs and outcomes, the first question we should ask is whether the program was intelligent enough to discriminate between the needs, preferences, and behavioral propensities of individual patients? Or did it just blast patients with messages and hope for the best? Even if the program was effective for a small population of patients (i.e., where it matched their unique characteristics), the beneficial effect is likely diluted beyond perception by the bulk of patients where the program did not fit.

In nonhealth care terms, if I want to advertise a new babysitting service, I may get some new business by putting flyers in 200 mailboxes. If I could send the same flyer to 200 minivan owners, I may get greater results. But if I could target people who have used babysitters within the past year (a behavior), we can safely predict that the response rate will likely be superior—those parents have already demonstrated through their behavior that they have discretionary money, they are willing to trust someone else with their children, etc. In so many cases, it is not the concept (disease management) or the program (diabetes intervention) that is broken; rather, it is how the program is deployed that produces the results. Customer analytics address this.

Given that we have not yet seen widespread adoption of customer analytics and shared insights across the health ecosystem, how confident can we be in the conclusions we have drawn to date about adherence? Consider that across our information systems today, there is an explicit "event trigger" that marks the start of a medication regimen: the writing of the prescription. In facilities where physicians use e-prescribing applications, the patient's prescription can simultaneously be sent to the patient's medical record and the patient's preferred local pharmacy for fulfillment. So if we wanted to explore medication adherence, the "start" of our investigation of each patient is when that electronic record is generated.

So when is the "end?" If the patient picks up month 1 of the prescription, but they fail to pick up month 2, is it really an adherence problem? Was the original diagnosis changed? Did adverse events force a drug change? Did the patient die? Did the patient move? Was the patient subsequently instructed to take half of the recommended dose, so they don't need the refill yet? Was the patient subsequently prescribed a required medication that contraindicated the first medication? Without collaboration around shared data and insights, we cannot effectively answer these questions.

BEYOND COMMERCIAL

It is such a simple question: why don't the patients get their medicine? And assuming we don't want to just call the patients to find out (which, cool technology aside, might be the best approach), there are multiple ways we can answer the question analytically. We could link their claims data to their electronic medical record (EMR) data to look for contraindications, adjusted diagnoses, and rapid follow-up visits. We could text mine the EMR data for dosing instructions. We could check for death records and address changes. We could check for care coordination contacts. We could investigate whether the patients' insurance plan and/or out-of-pocket expenses correlate with adherence. And assuming we identified an adherence problem, we could then test interventional programs designed to improve adherence—calls from case managers, email reminders, mobile alerts, adjusted co-pays, etc. But we could not definitively answer the question analytically unless we shared data and insights.

Returning briefly to Alexandria's library, one of the interesting but often under-discussed aspects of the library was *ad hoc* knowledge sharing. Within the literary works housed in the library, scholars would write their own notes and interpretations in the margins of the texts. These notes were available for the next reader to see, consider, and even contribute. Though today we might consider such acts vandalism, it was a beautiful technique at the time for disseminating knowledge and furthering academic explorations. It was open, multidisciplinary collaboration at its best.

Like all of the analytics scenarios we explore in this book, it is probably best to not classify customer analytics purely related to one set of questions like "commercial" (i.e., only pertaining to sales and marketing). As the adherence example above illustrates, many customer analytics scenarios operate across clinical, financial, administrative, and individual dimensions. And if we accept that there is a strong relationship between these different dimensions, any insights we derive will be constrained until we incorporate customer analytics.

CHAPTER **11**

Risk Management

RISKY BUSINESS

What exactly is risk? Across the health ecosystem today, the term "risk" can be used to characterize a wide variety of issues, as shown in Figure 11.1:

- **Health Risks**—the propensity for specific individuals or populations to manifest adverse clinical issues.

- **Financial Risks**—the revenue and cost exposure incurred by health payers, and increasingly providers, in treating an individual or population. Fraud, waste, and abuse fall into this category as well.

- **Safety Risks**—the propensity for individual health practitioners, departments, and institutions to commit or experience avoidable medical errors.

- **Quality Risks**—the propensity for individual health practitioners, departments, and institutions to deliver suboptimal care. This includes adverse event risks—the likelihood that a specific therapy will introduce undesirable effects in the patient.

- **Security Risks**—threats to the protection of staff, patients, information, assets, and continuity of business.

- **Reputation Risks**—threats to individual and corporate brands, public perceptions, and political climates.

167

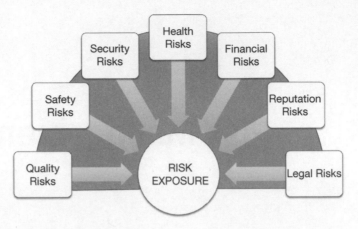

Figure 11.1 Sample Risk Factors.

- **Legal Risks**—threats related to litigation from other constituents, liability issues, and the loss of intellectual property.

Though it might be tempting to attempt to characterize these risk types as distinctive, the reality is that they are interdependent. For example, the realization of quality risks can immediately produce safety, health, reputation, and legal risks.

WHY ARE RISKS SO HARD?

The health and life sciences industries have dealt with risk for decades now. And yet, it still seems very—well, risky. Why is that?

Risks have three particularly undesirable characteristics:

1. Risk is often difficult to detect. Most risk inventories are the result of human brainstorming ("Let's think of all the risks and write them down"). But the human brain is not capable of foreseeing all of the different interacting effects that can produce risks in systems as complex as health care.

2. Risk is difficult to measure. There are two common ways risk is measured: subjectively by subject matter experts (i.e., how often does this happen, and how big of an impact does it create), or

more empirically through qualitative and quantitative research that usually assesses the prevalence of a single risk factor or small set of factors.

3. Risk is difficult to mitigate. How do you know if an intervention successfully reduces the probability or impact of a risk? Like risk detection and measurement, risk mitigation often results from brainstorming and limited research efforts, but the ability to link real-world results is often loose at best.

But despite these limitations, all risks have one universal trait that makes them a topic worthy of a health analytics discipline: every risk has at least one factor that has predictive power in the manifestation of the risk. And through the analytical study of these factors, we can improve health care.

RECHARACTERIZING RISK FACTORS

For the purposes of this book, we will define a risk factor as any measurable dimension that correlates with the prevalence, probability, severity, and impact of any risk. In other words, a risk factor is anything that positively or negatively covaries with or influences risk. In our use of the term, there is no assumption of causality; it does not matter whether the risk factor causes the risk or simply co-exists with the risk. The coexistence—in whatever form it takes—opens the door to prediction.

Examples of risk factors can include a wide variety of topics:

- **People.** Patient dimensions obviously impact risk: current health status, medical and family history, genomics, and many other factors. Physician dimensions also impact risk: the way individuals work, interact with patients, and practice medicine can be factors as well.

- **Organizations.** Institutions, practices, and departments can contain risk factors: policies, structures, geographic locations, culture, business models, pricing strategies, customer segmentation, and many more factors can mediate risk.

- **Medical Domain.** Some areas of medicine such as maternal fetal medicine are inherently more risky than others such as podiatry. Some diseases are more life-threatening than others, and individual diseases and disorders carry different risks with comorbidities.

- **Treatment.** Drugs and medical devices contain risk factors. So do surgeries, psychological interventions, dietary changes, treatment protocols, and hospitalization.

- **Activities.** The actions we take usually carry risk factors. Washing hands, for example, influences the prevalence of staph infections. Disease management programs, early interventions, the use of technologies, and the daily operating practices and procedures within an institution all manifest different sets of risk factors.

- **Data.** Our information can actually contain risk factors: data source, quality, timeliness, completeness, representativeness, and many other factors can influence risk. And within our data, of course, we find many risk factors: lab results routinely assess risk of disease, for example.

You may be able to think of even more than these. And in seeing this list, the natural tendency is to attempt to make a comprehensive list of risk factors: let's brainstorm! But the point is the exact opposite: a risk factor can be literally anything. Though brainstorming potential risk factors is useful, an even more useful approach is simply to look for where risks manifest, and analytically determine what sorts of factors covary with that risk. If we can let the data inform us more about risks, we stand a greater likelihood in investing our time and energy in the right risks and mitigations.

THE EXAMPLE OF CUSTOMER SEGMENTATION

Since risk management is such a huge issue for health payers, let's use an example from their market segment to illustrate the point.

Historically, health insurers have developed customer segments for use in their actuarial processes, pricing strategies, and disease management programs (among other business initiatives). A payer might, for example, group diabetic patients together in one risk pool and patients at risk for hip and knee replacements in another risk pool. In working with many payers over the years, one thing has become apparent: these customer segments are usually hypotheses. At some point, someone sat down and said, "Based on our view of the business, we think it makes the most sense to segment our risks into the following buckets." The segments, based most often on claims, lab, and prescription data, represent a fundamental aspect of profitability for every payer. And in articulating those specific segments, the underlying hypothesis is that the segmentation taxonomy (e.g., diabetics vs. hip-and-knee) is the best way to characterize and manage risk.

But that hypothesis is often untested—it may make logical sense, it may even be supported by an analysis of the data. But assuming the proposed taxonomy is a reliable way of segmenting risk, a question remains: is it the BEST way to characterize risk?

By expanding our data and analytical palette, we can often answer that question differently. New data sources allow us to assess the predictive strength of thousands of different variables on risk. Optimization algorithms then allow us to use those factors to construct segmentation models that deliver the best overall business value. The hypothesis—the new segmentation taxonomy—is derived directly from the observable world. And with more time, observations, and variables, the more powerful (and competitively advantageous) our risk management becomes.

RISK INTERDEPENDENCIES

Every constituency in health care—providers, life sciences firms, governments, payers, even patients and physicians—are in the risk management business. Consider:

- Out of every 10,000 promising drug compounds discovered, only one ever makes it to market. As a single drug's research program can easily top $1 billion with no certainty of safety, efficacy, regulatory approval, or payer formulary inclusion, pharmaceutical companies incur large quantities of financial risk.

- Providers face risk with every patient they see and every procedure they deliver. Sick people sometimes die. Accidents sometimes happen in caring for patients, and those accidents can have significant and tragic consequences. Care delivery is an inherently chaotic and unpredictable process, making the management of costs very challenging.

- Patients carry the biological and behavioral risks of disease, bankruptcy due to the costs of a serious chronic or life threatening illness in the family, and the risks of experiencing medical errors and adverse drug reactions.

As you look through these risks, notice that risks within one constituency directly impact the risks of other constituencies. Risks in health care are interdependent. Health risks are mediated by behavioral risks. Cost risks are mediated by health risks. Three examples that illustrate this point include:

1. Drugs with lots of adverse events not only impact pharmaceutical profitability and brand, they also manifest health risks in patients and escalate payer reimbursement costs.

2. Providers that cannot manage the risks of medical errors produce avoidable medical costs in their payers' risk pools and lower health outcomes in patients.

3. Payers that structure their businesses around suboptimal member segmentation reduce the opportunity for effective interventions, raising patient health risks and provider utilization.

So whether or not we can fully characterize the nature of any specific risk relationship (i.e., is it correlative or causal), we know there is an interacting effect. Accordingly, trying to manage any one risk in the absence of the others is a huge lost opportunity.

So at this point, we can summarize our risk discussion as follows:

- Risks are very difficult to detect, measure, and mitigate.

- All risks have at least one factor that is reliably predictive, but the factors could be almost anything.

- Our growing data repositories can point us towards what factors exist, and how important each factor might be.

- Risks among health constituents are interdependent; the mani-festation of a risk in one market has inevitable impacts on the other markets.

So how can our health ecosystem deal with risks more effectively?

EVERYBODY IN THE POOL

At the beginning of this book, we argued that health care must become collaborative in order to transform. As we look at risk management, the true implications of shared data and insights begin to emerge.

There is strength in numbers. Even though payers regularly pool risk as part of their business model, neither they nor other members of the health and life sciences industry have extended the concept of risk pooling across the breadth of risk domains we've discussed. Yet the opportunity for insight and innovative improvements is signifi-cantly stronger in a collective: more data; a much broader set of institutional and individual experiences; a more comprehensive inventory of assessable risk factors; and therefore a more thorough understanding of risk detection, measurement, and mitigation. When it involves multiple market segments, collaborations also serve to better illuminate the interdependencies in risk factors across constituents.

Some examples of shared data and insights we already see within the industry include the following:

- **Patient Safety Organizations.** The Patient Safety and Quality Improvement Act of 2005 created a type of organization focused on pooled insights. Patient safety organizations (PSOs) collect and analyze confidential information reported by providers related to quality and safety, such as medical errors. PSOs provide legal protection for the disclosure of quality and safety informa-tion, encouraging transparency and continuous improvement across the health ecosystem. Examples of PSOs include the World Health Organization's World Alliance for Patient Safety, the United Kingdom's National Patient Safety Agency, and more than 75 organizations listed by the U.S. Department of Health and Human Services' Agency for Healthcare Research and Quality (AHRQ).

■ **Drug Surveillance.** In 2007, Congress mandated that the U.S. Food and Drug Administration (FDA) create an active surveillance system for monitoring drugs. In response, the FDA launched the "Sentinel Initiative," a project focused on establishing a surveillance system for monitoring all FDA-regulated products. Combined with federal requirements for reporting adverse drug reactions to the FDA, the industry should eventually reap the benefits of more comprehensive views of drugs in the real world. And over time, hopefully, these views will evolve from retrospective reporting into predictive modeling and simulation.

■ **Clinical Trials Registries.** Though initially started as simply a site for collecting information about ongoing clinical studies, ClinicalTrials.gov in the United States is gradually becoming a site that inventories both clinical studies and their results. Other shared research repositories are also gradually standing up, offering unprecedented opportunities in reusability: meta-analyses, research repeatability, comparative effectiveness, and the identification of personalized medicine factors driving drug safety and efficacy.

■ **Open Innovation.** One of the most interesting and powerful shifts in the U.S. life sciences market over the past decade has been an increased willingness to collaborate on research that was once considered too competitively sensitive to involve multiple firms. Though the industry has a long way to go before true transparency occurs, pharmaceutical giants like Merck, GSK, Johnson & Johnson, and Sanofi have already launched "open innovation" initiatives that basically allow pharmaceutical companies to share risk.

Of course, no institution needs to wait for a large-scale or national initiative on shared data and insights. The ongoing proliferation of health information exchanges, consumer data aggregators, and clearinghouses for all sorts of health-related data means that organizations of all sizes and types can undertake improved approaches to risk management. Imagine for a moment the ability to measure risks in relation to others. What risks have they already seen that you have not seen yet? What risk factors were most predictive for them, and how does your organization differ along those factors? By scaling our experiences and insights more effectively, we increase our innovation velocity.

THE CATCH

If this new vision of risk management sounds too good to be true, you are right. Some risk factors will already exist in our data. Other risk factors will emerge when we join our data with nontraditional, external sources of data. Still others may be found in the data of other institutions, but not our own institution (i.e., we may not collect the data today). And others may defy an obvious way of even describing it—how would you represent corporate culture in electronic data, for example? So there is work to be done in learning how to collect and communicate risk factors, especially those that do not currently reside consistently in industry data models (e.g., HIPAA transaction sets, clinical documentation). And, of course, analytics can help with some of these challenges as well through data mining, factor analysis, and other techniques.

In short, the end game in risk management is the same; namely, using advanced analytics to help us:

- Identify real risks.
- Identify the risk factors associated with each risk.
- Characterize the interdependencies within and across risks and risk factors.
- Characterize the predictive strength of each risk factor—which factors exacerbate the risk, and which ones mitigate it.

By focusing our efforts closest to the real risks, we can ultimately reduce the prevalence, probability, severity, and impact of risks that most contribute to health outcomes and costs.

Use As Directed

As mentioned in Chapter 10, nonadherence to prescription medications is a huge issue across health care, impacting multiple areas of risk. To help firms more proactively manage these risks, one pharmacy benefits management company has developed a "better mousetrap" with predictive analytics.

The organization has developed predictive models for adherence based on data from over 400 different factors covering patients, physicians, drugs, conditions, and behavioral patterns. Patients who score low on adherence propensity are offered assistance based on the expected cause of the nonadherence: pill bottles with electronic timers, phone call reminders, automatic refill programs, additional medical education on their particular condition, and other interventions designed to mitigate the risks associated with nonadherence. They estimate effective adherence interventions save somewhere between $1,500 and $9,000 a year per patient.

RISK ADJUSTMENT

As U.S. health reform continues to unfold, risk modeling is actually taking on more of a direct impact in health organization revenue. Though a comprehensive review of changes in risk adjustment is beyond the scope of this book, it is important to point out the growing importance of health analytics in addressing this problem space. Plans, providers, and even life sciences firms (via comparative effectiveness) stand to benefit or lose based on how well risk is being characterized. Two focus areas include:

1. **Maximizing Reimbursement.** Plans and providers need to ensure that the data used and the compensation received reflect the world of health care in which they live. Risk assessment, data quality, risk monitoring, and reporting are all critical in managing risk and reimbursement in this context. For example, analytics can look at a patient's comprehensive data profile for risk factors that would otherwise indicate that the patient should be considered in a higher-risk reimbursement pool, but for

whatever reason the patient is not currently allocated to that pool (e.g., coding error, incomplete data, error in data aggregation). Analytics can also facilitate modeling of different risk adjustment methodologies for purposes of optimization.

2. **Influencing Reimbursement Policy.** Providers, payers, and life sciences firms will all benefit if risk adjustments reflect real-world experiences. To date, most risk adjustment policies and reimbursements have been derived from analyses of demographic, diagnostic, and claims data. Though useful, the goals of risk adjustment would be better served through more comprehensive modeling of risks, costs, behaviors, and interventions. Beyond simply "covering the gaps," risk adjustment could actually evolve to a real incentive for driving improved health outcomes at lower costs.

Of course, risk adjustment maturity depends on risk characterization maturity, and there is ample opportunity to grow our capabilities there as well.

Hidden Gems

As health organizations assume more risk for both health outcomes and financial reimbursement, it will be increasingly important that they take steps to ensure their patient populations are accurately reflected in reimbursement programs. For one large U.S. health insurer, that has meant making sure their Medicare reimbursements match the real risks within their member populations.

Electronic medical information is far from perfect: providers miscode conditions, members fail to receive medical services, and diagnoses are sometimes never captured. In order to ensure proper reimbursements, their analytics group developed an analytical model that can detect these data issues. By correlating hundreds of variables across more than two dozen medical condition groups, the program is able to both identify and prioritize (based on the size of potential reimbursement) patients that may have undiagnosed or unreported conditions. In addition to collecting millions of dollars of previously undetected reimbursement opportunities, the insights can also be used for proactive clinical interventions, marketing programs, and other forms of patient engagement. When risks are interdependent, better managing a single risk can help manage other risks as well.

BORROWING FROM OTHER INDUSTRIES

How do other industries work with risk? Is there an opportunity to "import" existing ideas into health care?

Let's look at one example. U.S. credit agencies have a mature framework for constructing credit risk profiles for individual consumers. Most U.S. consumers are at least tangentially familiar with credit scores. The FICO score, the most common credit-scoring model, uses a consumer's payment history, credit utilization history, and other factors to statistically derive a score that reflects the risk of default on a loan. Lenders routinely obtain a FICO score for the consumer prior to approving any new loan as part of their risk management process.

It may be a stretch to think that we could develop a single FICO-like score that would reasonably represent the diversity of a given consumer's health risks. But could more granular scores be developed that could easily communicate across organizational boundaries the risks carried by an individual. Would you need a person's private health information in order to derive the score?

In the summer of 2011, FICO announced that it would be calculating a Medication Adherence Score for 10 million U.S. consumers. Factors that FICO uses in scoring this risk include gender, marital status, family size, age, home ownership, automobile ownership, employment status, length of occupancy in current residence, and other factors. Note that FICO doesn't necessarily need access to a person's health records to score their medication adherence risk—other variables obtainable from public data sources are sufficiently reliable to predict a person's behavior. Though some consumers and industry experts may initially feel uncomfortable with the idea that a person's pill-taking behavior can be modeled and shared, the brutal reality is medication nonadherence is a $250 billion+ problem that results in avoidable hospital admissions, over 100,000 annual deaths, and decreased health outcomes for millions of patients. So it's hard to argue that a risk management intervention, if done properly, is not in everyone's best interest.

FICO is just one example of analytical risk management techniques developed in other industries—financial services, telecommunications, retail, hospitality—that can provide innovation within health care as well. Can portfolio optimization models from financial services help pharmaceutical companies more effectively manage their multibillion dollar research portfolios? Can behavioral propensity modeling from retail help payers more effectively engage high-risk patients in medical interventions and programs? Can providers learn about reducing financial risks associated with facility underutilization by looking at predictive analytics used by casinos and hotels?

GROWING RISKS

We are only scratching the surface of the topic of risk in health and life sciences. Outlier adjustments, condition and severity adjustments, risk corridors, payment risk analysis, and many more topics are taking a more central role in our industry's emerging discussions on how to improve outcomes and costs. One could argue quite accurately that Chapter 6 (financial performance) and Chapter 9 (behavioral medicine) were really about risk. That is the interdependent nature of the issues in this ecosystem.

As our health system evolves, every health organization is not just trying to manage risk—they are actively taking on new and different risks. Value-based contracting and accountable care models represent fundamentally different risk profiles as compared to volume-based business models. So developing new competencies in risk management has become more important than ever.

CHAPTER 12

Quality and Safety

DEFINING QUALITY

On February 7, 2003, a 17-year old girl named Jésica received a heart and lung transplant at one of the top health institutions in the United States. Unfortunately, the organs she received were from a patient of the wrong blood type. The young patient died two weeks later.

Jésica's story is not unique, and the unnecessary and tragic deaths that sometimes gain media attention are not the only illustrations of quality failures and inadequacies across health care. Hospital readmissions, medical errors, adverse drug events, hospital-acquired conditions—the inherent complexity in both service delivery and R&D practically breeds problems in safety, reliability, predictability, and consistency. Patients sometimes suffer unnecessarily while heath industry workers—many of whom chose to work in health care out of a sense of altruism—become increasingly frustrated with a system that at times seems incapable of honoring the medical profession's most basic tenet of doing no harm.

In an industry with such an obvious mandate for quality, it is surprising how ambiguously we define "quality." Depending on the person, institution, and context of discussion, quality in health care can cover a very broad palette of topics:

- **Outcomes**—"quality" can be used to characterize maximizing the overall clinical results achieved for a patient.
- **Engagement**—"quality" can refer to the nature of the interactions between providers and patients.

- **Satisfaction**—"quality" can refer to consumer sentiment of providers and payers.

- **Efficiency**—"quality" can refer to how efficiently health care is delivered.

- **Safety**—"quality" can refer to avoiding unintended consequences such as medical errors.

- **Utilization**—"quality" can refer to underuse, overuse, and misuse of medical services.

The ambiguity in defining quality is pervasive. For example, a single booklet by the Agency for Healthcare Research and Quality (AHRQ), "Guide to Health Care Quality: Know It When You See It," uses all of the above characterizations of quality. Yet despite the obvious lack of clarity, most of these quality areas are increasingly the subject of standardized metrics, reporting requirements, and public benchmarking.

This chapter avoids the somewhat religious-like debates of defining quality; the industry lacks consensus, and quality in any industry is subjective. It also avoids debating the relative merits of various quality improvement and management techniques (e.g., Lean, Six Sigma, Total Quality Management), though they are important as well. Instead, the intention is to characterize a more analytics-oriented view on quality. And it starts by suggesting that any definition of quality in health care should, at a minimum, include the following six attributes, as shown in Figure 12.1:

1. **Effective**—the right care is delivered.

2. **Safe**—the wrong care is not delivered.

3. **Efficient**—care is delivered without excessive time or costs.

4. **Measurable**—the assessment of quality must be quantifiable, even if the measurement itself is subjective, by assessing process execution and/or results.

5. **Reliable**—quality is only present if it can be consistently delivered.

6. **Defensible**—quality care is care supported by evidence.

And contrary to the current industry view, I am not suggesting that quality is equated to conformance with national standards or published best practices. Here is why.

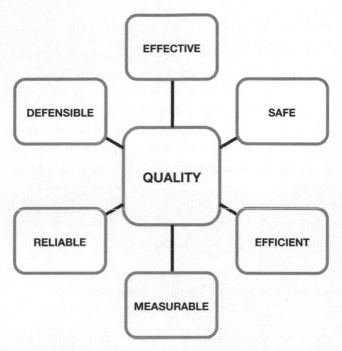

Figure 12.1 Six Minimum Attributes of Quality.

A Rose by Any Other Name

Regardless of whether industry consensus exists on the definition of quality, organizations are actively developing financial models based on it.

One Midwest health services organization scores each individual provider along two dimensions: quality and cost. To derive the quality score, the firm models nearly 90 different variables related to national practice standards, internal processes, and even customer satisfaction scores. To derive the cost score, the organization looks at both affordability and effectiveness measures. Though patients are always free to select their provider of choice, the organization actively steers patients towards high-scoring providers in hopes of delivering the best care at the best cost. Similar techniques are used to score patients who may benefit from health interventions like disease management programs. Leaders estimate that the combined effect of these analytical approaches has reduced yearly costs by over $125 million.

NOT YOUR FATHER'S TOYOTA

Current perceptions of quality improvement have developed from studying the manufacturing practices of companies like General Electric, Motorola, and Toyota during the last century. Those practices have largely focused on improving quality through reductions in process variance. For example, processes that operate with "Six Sigma quality" produce less than 3.4 defects per million. So a lot of attention is paid to assessing, documenting, measuring, and subsequently improving business processes.

There is absolutely no doubt that practice variation is harming patients and distorting health costs. One Dartmouth Atlas Project report[1] found massive inconsistencies purely on geography within a state:

- Two-fold variation for cardiac bypass surgery
- Two-fold variation in back surgery
- Three-fold variation in carotid endarterectomy (stroke prevention)
- Four-fold variation in coronary angioplasty
- Seven-fold variation in prostate transurethral resection

Some studies suggest that evidence-based care is provided less than 60% of the time. Data like this clearly illustrates that evidence-based decisions are not always operating. Accordingly, much of the attention on quality in health care has been focused on developing process definitions and performance criteria that establish a baseline from which process variation can be measured.

Some of the ideas presented in this book might be construed as throwing fuel on the practice variation fire. In multiple areas of the book, it is suggested or at least implied that existing "best practices" are likely not "best" whether they are "practiced" or not. Some practice variation should not only be expected, but those variations—when supported by analytical evidence—represent ways to optimize clinical outcomes and minimize costs. Why would that be true in health care, but not manufacturing?

Manufacturing quality principles are clearly useful, but they are founded on the idea that controlling process variation controls output variance. If a consistently performing machine is used in a highly consistent process, that machine should produce the same output time after time. Thus, if you control the process, you control the output.

The problem in health care is that the machines (i.e., the people) are not consistent. Saying that delivering the same clinical process will produce the same results does not reflect the natural variations inherent in patients, physicians, institutions, and cultures that also produce variations in that output. That is not to say that process controls are not important or useful—some of the issues that led to Jésica's failed transplants were absolutely process problems—but simply standardizing and measuring processes will not solve all of our quality issues. Conformance should not be the goal; controlled, evidence-based practice should be the goal.

ON TRACK

So if quality across health care is not delivered purely from manufacturing principles, where should we be looking to get quality improvements?

The first step in our search is acknowledging that our health processes are unavoidably chaotic. Chaotic in this sense does not mean wildly uncontrolled or undisciplined; rather, it means subject to unpredictable variables. Differences abound, and we will not eliminate all of them. So we should develop strategies and business plans that anticipate this variability, and give us more capabilities in managing our performance through the variability. So where have we learned management and prediction of chaos?

One example of chaotic systems would, of course, be the weather. Through predictive modeling and simulation, science can produce relatively accurate predictions of what the weather will be in a particular location on a particular day. As that day approaches, our predictive accuracy increases, never reaching 100% but certainly reaching "good enough" for most situations. And whereas our weather predictions correlate strongly with historical weather patterns for that location and time of year, the predictive model itself is driven by conditions as they are emerging in the real world.

As I am writing this chapter, I am sitting on a back porch in rural North Carolina. It is January, and the average temperature for this region in January is between 51°F (high) and 30°F (low). With temperatures in that range, you might wonder why I would be sitting outside writing a book. But today's high was 75°F, and right now it is very comfortable. It is almost never that warm here in January, but it has been as high as 80°F in the past. It has also been as cold as −6°F, so there is a variance of almost 90 degrees in our historical data.

Given that, no one would have ever been able to accurately and reliably predict today's temperature by looking at these historical temperatures, just as it is very difficult to predict how a given individual's health will evolve based purely on population research. Even three weeks ago, no one would have been able to call today's weather. But three days ago, analytics predicted today's temperature to within three degrees of accuracy. It also accurately predicted the cloud cover, humidity, chance of rain, wind speeds, and a plethora of other conditions that gave me confidence in opting to work on this chapter on the porch. Analytics give us the capabilities necessary to manage the otherwise chaotic nature of weather.

Another example of chaos management is war. Over the centuries, militaries have learned how to navigate the highly unpredictable nature of battlefields. Concepts such as command and control, communication, situational awareness, and responsiveness are all crucial to effectively managing a military campaign. And military strategists study prior battles—their own and others—in order to learn how to improve both strategy and tactics when encountering the enemy. Today, care coordination programs are slowly coming to embrace some of these ideas (e.g., accountability, communication), but much more work is needed, especially in the areas of individual differences (i.e., fighting an enemy that looks like this one) as opposed to population trends (i.e., general fighting tactics).

A third example is racing. Though a racetrack is a highly stable piece of infrastructure, the cars and drivers on that track are not. Equipment specifications, operating configuration, wind, rain, driver errors, and even chance all come into play before reaching the finish line. Through communications, equipment readings, and physical inspections during pit stops, both drivers and crews are constantly monitoring engine performance, tire condition, fuel levels, track conditions, real-time performance changes (i.e., hot tires stick to the track better than cold ones) and many other factors that collectively determine if and how a car and her team finish an event. And based on the performance, the team learns how to perform better at the next event.

Both militaries and race teams have process controls such as standard procedures that help ensure quality. A pit crew changing the tires of a racecar is a testament to process management. But the teams use a lot more than that. The German military strategist Helmuth von Moltke is frequently credited with the phrase "no plan survives first contact with the enemy." We must be able to observe, respond, and adapt based on the rapidly evolving conditions on the ground. So our goal in health quality should be two-fold: control process variation where useful, but also empower more adaptive teams.

AVOIDING THE OBVIOUS

When I first started working in the provider market, I was confused by the industry's use of the term "quality." Coming from the pharmaceutical market segment, quality had some very specific meanings related to issues like standardized procedures, quality controls, and compliance. Yet in health care, it seemed to mean all that and more: safety, health outcomes, and performance management, to name a few. Over time, I've come to appreciate both perspectives on quality, and they are both right. And wrong. I strongly agree with the concepts of measurement and process control. But I also agree with the concepts of evidence and agility.

When I set out to write this book, I had originally thought of doing a chapter on quality and safety where I summarize the ecosystem's current status on metric calculations. But the more I worked on the book, the more I felt bothered by two things related to quality. The first issue was that of timeliness—by the time the book went to print, any objective summarization of quality metrics would be out of date. That I could live with, but the second issue was more significant to me. Many others before me have written chapters like that, and to be honest, I don't like any of the ones I've read. To me, they always seem to be missing the point.

WE JUST HAVE TO DO THIS

I was once asked to help improve the productivity and quality of a software development team focused on clinical applications. The impression from the executives was that it was taking way too long to get things done: fix software emerging bugs, add critical features, improve system performance, etc. It was taking many months to get a basic bug fix released, and multiple years to develop new features. As I began my investigation, my initial hypothesis was that there might be some missing skills in the organization; if I could identify the skill gaps, I could close the gap to get the improvements the organization needed. But that hypothesis turned out to be wrong.

The team actually had great skills—some of the best I had seen. They also had great passion, commitment, ideas, a strong work ethic, and many other high-performing team attributes. They also knew exactly what needed to be built, and were working feverishly day and night to get it done. So why wasn't their performance on par?

As I started to dig further, it became obvious that the team was investing very heavily in process control and documentation, which in many software development environments would be considered a good thing. Except in this case, even a minor bug fix would generate hundreds of pages of documentation, and a major release was usually much more than that. In looking at their "quality system" (as it is often termed), they had many documented processes. They had processes defining how they developed their products. They had processes defining how they created processes. They had processes that checked that their processes were operating properly. They had a regular maintenance schedule for their processes. Every process was documented, and every process produced documentation. In the midst of some of the most sophisticated computing infrastructure for miles, this organization had paper literally falling off the shelves. And when asked why they were generating so much documentation, the answer was, "Because this is a regulated system, we have to do this. Customers and the FDA demand it."

The question no one appeared to be asked was why? Why would the FDA and customers want documentation like this? What was the intention behind creating the documentation? The answer is not that people wanted vast quantities of paper (well, at least most people don't). Customers and regulators actually wanted evidence of quality. The goal was not supposed to be the paper—the goal was supposed to be quality itself.

Over time, the original intention got washed over with traditions, myths, and cultural norms that were actually inhibiting accomplishing the quality goal. If an important software system is found to have a defect (an inevitable situation in all software) and a solution is known, does it make sense to use the defective software for months and months out of a concern for quality control? Process and change controls are obviously needed to preserve the existing quality attributes of the system, but there is a point of diminishing returns.

The other question that was not getting much attention was "What do they do with this information?" Assuming that the team could produce this paper on demand, what happened next? In this case, the answer was "Nothing." The important thing to the customer was knowing that evidence existed, but they didn't actually do anything with the information. If that is the case, then the form and structure of the evidence should be irrelevant, so the obvious question then becomes "Do we really need all this paper, or are there other ways to generate evidence of a quality process?"

I learned from that exercise to always ask follow-up questions when I hear someone say "We just have to do this." That phrase can be a sign that an organization or individual has reduced actual business intentions into blind policies and expectations; they may not appreciate "why" things are being done, or what is supposed to happen next. And if they don't understand these two things, they can't make effective decisions in the best interest of the organization.

THE GROWING INVENTORY

Today, health care quality metrics are moving at a rapid rate towards "We just have to do this." There appears to be no limit to the number of metrics we should track, and there appears to be no limit to the number of organizations entitled to impose more metrics. And the evidence supporting any particular metric or performance criteria seems at times uncertain at best.

At the time of this writing, the Agency for Healthcare Research and Quality (AHRQ) listed 7,402 measures in the National Quality Measures Clearinghouse covering:

- Diseases and conditions (2,427)
- Treatments and interventions (4,494)
- Administration (481)

The Department of Health and Human Services maintains a separate database of over 2,000 quality measures. The most recent Joint Commission (TJC), formerly the Joint Commission on Accreditation of Healthcare Organizations (JCAHO), core measure sets is contained in a zip file consisting of over 100 individual files, each spelling out numerous measures. The National Center for Quality Assurance adds another 75 Healthcare Effectiveness Data and Information Set (HEDIS) measures plus an inventory of various endorsed metrics.

So before a health organization enters any value-based contracts (which by definition contain quality and performance measures), they face the task of sorting through and adopting a growing inventory of literally thousands of measures. Even eliminating redundancy across the measures, a given institution could easily be on the hook for well over 1,000 performance and quality metrics. Facing this reality, three questions every health leader today should be asking are:

1. Is it feasible for a given institution to effectively measure and manage over 1,000 measures?

2. Is it realistic to think that thousands of measures are all critical to a given organization's success?

3. How do you know what is important?

Both logic and experience suggest that it is not possible or practical to effectively manage thousands of measures. And even if it were possible, it likely wouldn't be cost effective. For a given organization, all of those measures are not equally important. Differences in patient populations, physician populations, disease prevalence, competitive differentiators, practice competencies, socioeconomic, and many other factors suggest that organizational leaders should be discriminative in selecting which metrics are important for their particular organizations.

Some metrics will always be required, and rightly so. But good strategy requires more than that. In his widely cited 1996 *Harvard Business Review* article "What is Strategy?," Michael Porter proposed that "the essence of strategy is choosing what not to do." Organizations must make trade-offs, and any organization attempting to take on an unfocused metric strategy risks:

- Draining resources from higher clinical priorities
- Diluting organizational attention from more competitively and financially sensitive focus areas (i.e., mission-critical)
- Fostering a lack of confidence in management expectations
- Increasing the demand on technical resources and infrastructure costs
- Inhibiting the development of a better performance-oriented culture via more successful performance management approaches

Said more simply, an unfocused metrics strategy escalates costs and increases financial risk.

STRATEGY AND PERFORMANCE MANAGEMENT

Many health organizations are currently using a "bottom-up" strategy for performance management. The inventory of metrics—either those easily available, or those explicitly requested via policies and contracts—determine what and how performance is measured.

But formalized frameworks for performance management have been widely implemented in other industries, and (when implemented properly) have been shown to be effective in improving both individual and organizational performance. Of these frameworks, Kaplan's "balanced scorecard" has garnered the most attention in recent years[2] (see Figure 12.2). But there is no "one size fits all" for performance management, and leaders implementing any form of formalized performance management are moving in the right direction.

The popularity of the balanced scorecard has been accompanied by the term "scorecard" being applied to almost anything related to reporting. Business intelligence tools that provide Web-based reports, sometimes employing graphical gauges, color coding, or other visually

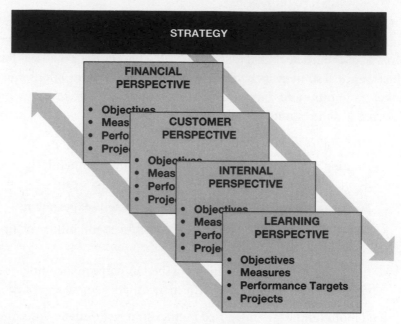

Figure 12.2 Typical Balanced Scorecard Framework.
Source: Adapted from Kaplan and Norton's model.

appealing objects, often describe their user interfaces as scorecards. In the context of our discussion here, those reporting tools are not considered performance management, as nothing is being managed.

The discipline of strategy and performance management helps organizations decide and manage what is important. They explicitly capture the goals and objectives of an organization, not just acceptable ranges of various measures. These goals and objectives are then linked to specific projects within the organization aimed at driving improvements that are aligned to the strategy. Measures and indicators then give leaders and managers both strategic and operational insights into current and expected performance. In institutionalizing the strategy, objectives, and performance criteria in this way, leaders are in effect agreeing what not to do.

TRANSPARENCY AND BENCHMARKING

One of the advantages to using strategy and performance management analytics, especially at the enterprise level, is that organizations begin to institutionalize their definitions and measurements. When everyone is looking at the same scorecard, they can make decisions from the same set of information.

All quality and safety metrics should be enterprise-wide assets. In order to make that a reality, those metrics need to be implemented in an analytical environment that is accessible to anyone associated with the institution. That analytical environment also serves as a management environment for the ever-increasing inventory of measures. As a source of metric formalization, strategic performance management environments aid in the organizational governance of performance measurement. The definitions, measurements, calculations, and results serve as the "source of truth" available to everyone.

This level of transparency is uncomfortable to many leaders. One concern is that the information might be used in inappropriate ways. The information presented might also be misinterpreted. And particularly in areas where performance is below desired levels, people may reject the information as inaccurate, skewed, or otherwise not indicative of the actual business processes.

These are all valid concerns. But they are also management issues. The concept of transparency cannot be applied only when the news is good and the audience is safe. It is important to acknowledge that the presentation of those risks is a good thing, as it provides a clear sign to management where additional education, cultural change, and continuous improvement might be needed in order to actually drive change. It is not desirable, but it is better to see it and fix it than to continue to operate as if it doesn't exist. And it is always better if you do it to yourself than when it is done to you.

To that end, one of the biggest reasons that organizations should be pursuing enterprise-wide performance management analytics is that other people and organizations will be monitoring their performance going forward. When quality metrics are relegated to individual reports spread across the organization, it is very difficult for managers to effectively manage organizational risk. Strategic performance management provides much stronger assurances that the right information will end up in front of the right people in a timely manner, especially when those performance metrics are coupled with alerting functionality to provide notification of concerning metrics.

For this reason, an organizational implementation of a metric should reflect industry consensus around its definition and derivation—a situation that creates internal challenges when industry-level quality definitions do not reflect the realities of a particular institution. Nevertheless, organizational leaders need to see what others will be seeing, even if it means creating two different measures of the same core issue. One effect of this transparency can be a health care variation of the "observer effect" in physics: the act of measuring a dimension can improve it.

As we achieve more transparency across the industry, enterprise performance measures should also unlock a new analytical opportunity: predicting the impact of changing care patterns. Today, adjustments to care practices are somewhat unpredictable because we lack performance data. Over time, though, the enterprise-level assets we develop from performance management will be leveraged to better predict how these changes impact both individual and organizational performance.

Keeping Score

CASE STUDY

Can organizations really culturally shift to take advantage of performance analytics?

One large U.S. teaching hospital uses a strategy map and balanced scorecards to provide this sort of transparency. The organization chose to focus on several core areas for improvement, including service excellence, quality of care, and financial performance. Their implementation tracks a wide variety of performance measures covering topics as diverse as length of stay, readmissions, mortality rates, patient satisfaction, infection rates, medical errors, and census and occupancy data. In providing access to this information to executives, physicians, and staff, one executive described the organization's approach as embedding "scorecards, analytics, and business intelligence into the fabric of the organization."

Did it work? By better focusing priorities, attention, and resources against the strategy map and scorecard, the institution saw a five-fold increase in operating margins, and their customer satisfaction peer ranking moved from the 40th to the 90th percentile.

SETTING QUALITY TARGETS

Summarizing the chapter so far, the major propositions covered are:

1. Regardless of any formal definition, quality in health care should be characterized by effective, safe, efficient, measurable, reliable, and defensible care.

2. Quality and safety improvements in health require us to acknowledge the need for both process controls as well as unpredictable emerging conditions.

3. When we pursue quality measurement, we need to be constantly assessing why we are doing the measurements, and what happens with the information we are gathering.

4. The industry is propagating way too many quality measures to effectively manage, so we need to focus.

5. Strategy and performance management frameworks offer us both techniques and analytical tools to connect #3 and #4.

In looking at how the industry is setting quality measures and targets, it is important to acknowledge five additional points that should influence our quality analytics.

1. Most measures today are purely descriptive and are not used for inferential statistics or predictive models. Said another way, the sophistication of our quality data science is too often constrained to counts, averages, and percentages. Whereas descriptive statistics are useful, unless we are pursuing more sophisticated approaches to forecasting and predicting performance measures, many of these quality metrics offer limited long-term utility. They begin to feel more like something "we just have to do."

2. The application of advanced analytics gives us the opportunity to understand one critical dimension that existing quality measures usually do not: causality. We do not want to just know a bad thing is happening—we want to know why. What are the conditions that are producing the negative outcome or measure? These insights require linking our quality analytics to the other analytical scenarios covered in this book.

3. One set of clues related to causality analysis may be found in analytically exploring the covariability in quality measures. Quality and performance metrics themselves can be a formal unit of study. Which ones actually seem to correlate most strongly with health outcomes and costs? Which ones do not? And what patterns emerge across metrics—can a change in one metric predict changes in other metrics, for example?

4. The opportunities in all of the above suggest a better science in selecting, defining, establishing performance criteria around, and evaluating health quality measures. Just because a measure makes logical sense should not be sufficient justification for institutionalizing the routine measurement. And research lacking predictive evidence (demonstrated analytically) should not be used to establish policies regarding quality measurement and standards of care. Quality measurement is not free; unless we plan to further contribute to the escalating costs of care, we need more evidence-based evaluation of quality measurement.

5. As our adoption of quality and performance standards grows, it will be increasingly important to link those analytics more closely to workflow. One obvious mechanism for doing that is alerting—sending messages or other notifications to people or systems when a measurement exceeds a predefined threshold, for example. Over time, though, alerting will be overwhelming (in some institutions, it may be already). In lieu of simply propagating more alerts, a more constructive approach may be quality and performance triage. In this approach, analytics help determine the clinical and financial severity of performance variations. If you believe that not all measures are created equal, analytics can help: a) discern which ones are more important, and b) operationally guide practitioners to focus on the things that matter most.

Of course, quality and safety issues are not purely the concern of providers and plans. Whether assessing manufacturing quality, clinical data quality, or many other quality dimensions, life sciences firms have a strong mandate for quality improvements as well. And one of the most important is in the area of drug safety.

DRUG SAFETY

Pharmaceutical organizations today routinely collect drug safety information in the form of adverse events experienced during clinical research. This data, as well as safety information collected once a drug is on the market, is routinely submitted to the FDA using standardized forms that collect enough basic information to characterize the observation as an adverse event. The FDA's Sentinel project has the goal of establishing a national electronic product safety surveillance system. Though progress in creating a production-class system has been slow and elusive, progress has been made on nearly a dozen topics, as well as a "mini-Sentinel" initiative, that have demonstrated the feasibility and value of such safety oversight.

Though the collected safety data is useful for regulatory reporting, it is much less useful for asking predictive questions about product safety. The Sentinel project has addressed this issue by *post hoc* data collection on a per-issue basis as needed. Such a process is: a) time consuming when not automated, b) not easily scalable across large numbers of products, and c) always reactive.

If, however, adverse event reports routinely triggered a brief follow-up questionnaire to medical staff that captured a broader set of information about the patient and the experience, then advanced analytics could likely develop predictive models that could prevent subsequent at-risk patients from experiencing these effects. Whereas these analyses might have the undesirable consequent of reducing product revenue (i.e., through warnings, label changes, and treatment guidelines), those lost revenues could be offset by greater future revenues in superior products developed through richer insights into each drug's mechanisms of action.

Through a more disciplined study of adverse events, the "exceptions" (i.e., patient characteristics that correlate with adverse events) enable us to better understand the "rules" (i.e., how and why the drug behaves in the real world). Whether such supplemental data collection and analysis were managed through industry-wide work involving the FDA, or through company-specific initiatives, the insights derived could serve the three goals of improving health outcomes, reducing costs, and driving medical innovations. And there are obvious opportunities to collaborate with providers and payers in this space, especially as it relates to data sharing and mining of clinical and claims data.

The hesitancy in more ambitious analytical explorations of drug safety has also spanned into the use (or lack thereof) of social media and other public data sources, both structured and unstructured. The industry has avoided mining these data repositories looking for signals because the detection of a signal or safety issue may obligate the company to report the finding to regulators and potentially compromise revenue. Yet the value in such data mining efforts is quite clear. Public data sources offer another view—and in many cases, a near real-time view—into a product's performance in the real world. The development of Patient Safety Organizations (PSOs) within the provider market space offers a model for how the drug industry may be able to avoid some of these risks.

THE BURDEN OF INSIGHT

In summary, health analytics can have a transformative impact on our understanding of quality and safety across the health ecosystem. Through advanced analytics, we can:

- Define what quality actually means for an organization through consistently deriving quality measures accessible to all constituents.

- Triage our inventory of measures to those most important, and link specific quality and safety measures to organizational strategy.

- Explore the causal relationships of quality and safety impairment through inferential statistics.

- Inform leaders, managers, and front-line staff what quality issues are actually important today, and which ones are emerging.

- Develop alerting systems for quality-related issues, and even automate quality improvement interventions.

- Mitigate the risks that external organizations may uncover things that the organization does not see.

But if these insights are attainable, with how much vigor should we pursue them? What are we getting ourselves into?

Spider-Man, the popular Marvel Comics superhero, first appeared in a comic book in August of 1962. In the story of his origin, Peter Parker acquires his enhanced abilities but does nothing to intervene in a nearby robbery. The criminal subsequently kills Peter's uncle, and the story concludes with a value lesson that "with great power comes great responsibility." For the next fifty years of comic book history, the idea that a person's ability to help morally obligates the person to act has become a central tenet of the Spider-Man mythos.

Radioactive spiders and philosophical debates notwithstanding, it is difficult to argue that we are following the first tenet of the Hippocratic oath when we know our inactions are propagating problems and we do not take the required steps to rectify it. Whether the issue is drug safety or medical errors or any of the other numerous quality and safety issues, the industry is called to a higher moral obligation. Those uncomfortable feelings we get each time we hear of a bad patient experience are reminders; if we can answer the question "Could we have done something?" with at least a "Maybe," then maybe we should be doing it already.

We sometimes dance around the question: is ignorance of a problem a reasonable defense? This is not an abstract, philosophical question. One of the things analytics accomplishes is reducing ignorance, so we need to be prepared for the responsibilities and burdens of insights.

NOTES

1. Brownlee, S., Weinberg, J., Barry, M. et al. (2011). "Improving Patient Decision-Making in Health Care: A 2011 Dartmouth Atlas Report Highlighting Minnesota." Dartmouthatlas.org
2. Kaplan, R. and Norton, D. (1986). "The Balanced Scorecard: Translating Strategy into Action," *Harvard Business School Press*.

CHAPTER **13**

The New Research
and Development

RETURNING TO ALEXANDRIA

Though the great library at Alexandria is a common subject in world history classes, the city's role in medicine is sometimes underrated. Among many philosophers, historians, mathematicians, and early scientists, Alexandria was home to Herophilos, a man that set a great example for our health analytics discussion: he saw untapped sources of information, and took on the challenging and exciting journey to new insights.

At the time of Herophilos, cultural and religious barriers precluded the dissection of human cadavers. But as a growing seat of knowledge, Alexandria was one of the few places in the ancient world that allowed dissection. Herophilos' willingness to take on these unconventional investigations enabled him to achieve astounding things in the service of science and medicine. He identified the brain as the seat of intellect, correcting Aristotle in the process. He opened the door to a new-and-improved scientific discipline of anatomy, and is credited with discovering the ovum. And continuing work started by his predecessor Hippocrates, Herophilos helped formalize the controlled investigative approach known today as the scientific method.

For the next two millennia, the scientific method served as man's most powerful instrument for developing our understanding of the universe and its mysteries. Through the scientific method, mankind has gradually replaced myth with fact and snake oils with antibiotics. Today, the average human life expectancy is 3–4 times greater than in Herophilos' time.

Around 2,300 years later, in March of 1996, a well-known Cornell University scientist named Dr. Carl Sagan published a book called *The Demon-Haunted World: Science as a Candle in the Dark*. His goal in the book was to highlight how science and the scientific method have contributed, and continue to contribute, to the advancement of mankind in ways far more accurate and impactful than alternative forms of conjecture about the nature of the world around us. Though offering hundreds of pages of evidence and commentary incontrovertibly demonstrating the value of scientific inquiry, Sagan also acknowledges:

> Science is far from a perfect instrument of knowledge. It's just the best we have . . . Science invites us to let the facts in, even when they don't conform to our preconceptions . . . every time we test our ideas against the outside world, we are doing science.

The 21st century will add to our arsenal of knowledge instruments.

THE END OF THEORY

In June of 2008, a writer for *Wired* magazine named Chris Anderson wrote a story called "The End of Theory: The Data Deluge Makes the Scientific Method Obsolete." In it, Anderson proposed that we have an alternative to traditional science in the form of "big data" and analytics.

To understand Anderson's point, consider for a moment the development of the scientific method. For the past few centuries, mankind has relied on this fairly specific framework for understanding the world around us. After thousands of years of groping in the dark for insights that all too often did not stand up to scrutiny, our species has broadly adopted a systematic, iterative method of hypothesis generation, testing, observation, and analysis that has produced an explosion of human advancement across all disciplines of science.

One reason that the scientific method has worked is that it produces data. When our scientific explorations began, we had no data. In a desert of data, every drop of water counts, and the scientific method was a water maker. And in contrast to eras where data was derived by individual (and therefore unavoidably biased) observations, the scientific method created a way of collecting data suitable for interpretation by multiple individuals using techniques less susceptible to bias. It even gave us a language for defining the boundaries of our interpretations— you could say that the water was pretty clean (or at least cleaner).

Fast forward to today, and we are drowning in data. Everyone owns a proverbial water maker, and both water jugs and filters are relatively inexpensive and getting cheaper. We are still thirsty; we have not mastered the art of drinking all of this water. But the water itself is rapidly becoming a commodity.

So Anderson's premise, though controversial to many, is simple: in a world where massively growing volumes of data and powerful analytics allow us to directly observe and measure the world in its natural state, do we still need the arbitrary "middle man" of the scientific method? In older times when we had no access to data that we could readily analyze to determine what is likely to happen in the real world, the scientific method offered us a repeatable, reliable framework for developing theories that predict the behavior of the world around us. Theories were our only path to prediction.

But today that is not true. We can directly observe the real world, gather data, and develop predictive models without any theoretical basis for those models. When a company compares the click-through performance of two different advertisements on the Web, analytics may show that more potential customers click on the second advertisement than the first. The company may not know why—it could be the font, color, language, size, or any number of factors. But the marketing leader doesn't need to know why in order to decide to use the second advertisement; it works better, so use it.

The scientific method is not the only way of growing our understanding of the world around us. And though it has been the most successful, the scientific method is certainly not the fastest. The controls that it mandates—while critical to a full understanding of the nature of the medical universe—are not always necessary to get to decisions that are not only "good enough," but may actually be better than the ones suggested by controlled scientific research.

Consider online patient communities. If normative disease treatment could evolve based on the online interactions among thousands of patients—for example, if we could see in their data that patients who are taking an alternative treatment path are experiencing statistically significant benefits over their peers—how much does it matter that this result did not originate from a controlled research study? You could argue that the patient sample may not be representative of patients at large. But we can already say definitively that controlled study participants are definitely not representative of patients at large: limited sample sizes, inclusion/exclusion criteria, etc. So which is more representative—the group of online patients, or the group of patients in the controlled study? The answer is we don't know. But we can reasonably predict based on data that path B seems to produce superior results for some patients, and that knowledge may be enough.

Of course, "predicting" and "understanding" are two different things. Whereas analysis of real-world data may allow us to develop predictive capabilities, it does not necessarily progress our understanding of why things work a certain way. For that, we still need the scientific method.

Practically, this shift represents a cultural and cognitive change for many researchers. Traditionally, scientists and statisticians have been taught to constrain "peeking" at data outside the context of rigorously controlled hypothesis testing, as such visibility can bias study design, execution, analysis, and interpretation. But under the "alternate" view of research described here, "peeking" is not only allowed, it is required (see Figure 13.1). Our data investigations are actually how we start the process of medical research, not just how we end it.

This "alternate" view is not so different as it might first appear to some. We have always pursued meta-analyses, observational studies, registries, and many other forms of research that are less constrained by experimental controls. The real difference going forward is that the emphasis on these types of research activities will increase. We have a large and growing base of data from which we can begin all sorts of research, and that research can move at a speed much faster than traditional models of controlled clinical research.

Of course, this new opportunity and speed has a trade-off. The challenge in advancing human knowledge in the 21st century will not

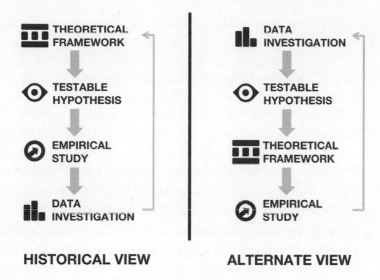

Figure 13.1 Historical Versus Alternate Views of Investigation.

be a lack of data: rather, the challenge is that the overwhelming proportion of data is not collected using the discipline of a scientific method, so the "boundaries" of our interpretation of the data are undefined. In our water metaphor, we have no idea what sorts of contaminants might be in our water, or in anyone else's water who might be willing to share it with us. So we need to get good at water treatment and handling.

Regardless of which approaches we choose to adopt—traditional science or big data investigations—the goals of improving our research and development (R&D) are largely the same.

GOALS OF A NEW RESEARCH MODEL

Most industry experts would acknowledge several major shortcomings in our current R&D and translational science efforts. It can take ten years to get "from bench to bedside." It takes around ten years and more than $1 billion to develop a new drug therapy. The odds of a newly discovered drug candidate eventually becoming a commercial product are around 10,000 to 1. The real-world behavior of new drug therapies often differs from what is observed experimentally (i.e., side effects, complications, safety concerns).

Accordingly, we believe there are five fundamental goals to improving R&D.

1. **Cost effective.** Today, the high expenses we incur in R&D produce expensive medical therapies. We need more efficient and cost-conscious ways of uncovering medical insights. The increasingly global nature of business and science offer us obvious opportunities in cost arbitrage, though we need to be conscious of potential geographical sampling bias in our clinical data. But beyond cheaper labor forces, the way we work needs to be more efficient and fiscally responsible.

2. **Timely.** Whether in the form of new drug therapies or modified treatment plans, we should not accept waiting a decade or more for medical improvements. Not only do we prolong human suffering, we also escalate the costs of both development and delivery.

3. **Risk balanced.** We should not risk billions of R&D dollars for products and therapies that are ultimately ineffective or unsafe. More importantly, though, our acceptance of risks—inherent to all R&D efforts—should be balanced. There will be places where we incur more risk for more potential reward, and other places where we are less risk tolerant. But our decisions should be intentional and driven by data.

4. **Personalized.** Medical treatments are not "one size fits all," and there is absolutely no reason that we should continue to operate as if we don't know that to be true. When a patient receives a suboptimal treatment, that patient experiences suboptimal results: decreased health outcomes, increased adverse events, increased complications, and increased risks and costs. That situation should be unacceptable to everyone, especially since we know it is avoidable.

5. **Reusable.** We need better utility from the data we collect. The common practice of shelving research data after its initial use severely limits our research velocity and insights, and contributes to lost opportunities for health improvement.

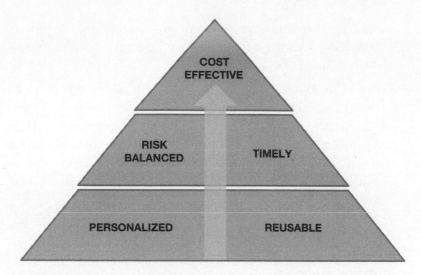

Figure 13.2 R&D Improvement Goals.

As shown in Figure 13.2, these goals for a new research agenda are very synergistic. If we are more effective in reusing our data assets, then the timeliness of our insights should be improved, and the costs associated with attaining those insights should be reduced. Likewise, if we aggressively pursue a more personalized approach to medical treatment, those insights should enable us to better manage risks and costs.

So with these five synergistic goals in mind, we can begin to develop a new paradigm for research, one that addresses the limitations of our existing model but also captures some of the new opportunities in data and technology.

CHARACTERISTICS OF A NEW RESEARCH PARADIGM

We believe any new model of R&D should have 10 specific attributes:

1. **Collaborative.** No research institution, public or private, academic or commercial, will have enough of the right information to drive timely, effective, and efficient innovation. Instead, we

must build cultures that facilitate cross-institutional sharing of knowledge—knowledge that at one time may have been considered competitively confidential.

2. **Reusable Data.** We need to proactively design research and collect data in ways that facilitate the subsequent reuse of that information. Companies invest a lot of time and money collecting clinical and operational data. When used more extensively across the health ecosystem with advanced analytics such as modeling and simulation, that data should be a diamond mine for making informed, predictive decisions.

3. **Process Optimized.** The manual efforts of the past—data collection, manipulation, quality adjustment, analysis, and performance improvement—need to be automated. Further, our efforts in innovative science should include innovations in the processes of doing the science, not just the science itself.

4. **Observational.** Results from tightly controlled experiments should be augmented with "real world" data investigations that can both guide more informed research designs, as well as explore issues that cannot be easily investigated experimentally in a timely and/or cost efficient manner.

5. **Consumer-Centric.** We should not settle for drugs when we know product and service combinations produce superior results. We should not let high R&D costs drive price when consumer markets can better manage the economics. We should not "settle" for treatments when patients want cures. And we should not expect patients to be disconnected from either their care or ongoing research.

6. **Predictive.** From the top levels of research programs all the way down to the attributes of individual studies within a single research program, predictive analytics should be used to anticipate and improve business planning, process efficiency, and clinical effectiveness.

7. **Real Time.** There is very little reason why data collection and analysis needs to be asynchronous. From electronic medical records to telehealth applications to real-time safety surveillance

systems to remote medical devices, R&D of medical therapies should be happening at the speeds modern technology support.

8. **Tailored.** The new marketplace requires differentiated treatments. It's time for life sciences organizations to use the opportunities enabled by 21st-century science—innovative technologies and deeper insights into the fundamental mechanisms of action associated with medical conditions that empower personalized medicine—to reestablish a curative mission in developing therapies that eradicate disease and medical disorders in both broad-based and niche populations.

9. **Profitable.** Better treatments should mean a better bottom line; treatments that make a difference in patients' can drive strong financial performance and brands. By applying advanced analytics to truly understand treatment portfolios, their corresponding safety and efficacy profiles, and how they work in different individuals, both patient and corporate health improves.

10. **Lifecycle-Oriented.** We have moved beyond the point where preclinical, clinical, and commercial considerations can be considered in isolation at different points in time. Advanced analytics give life sciences organizations the ability to validate a treatment candidate's scientific and commercial potential through smart integration of complex data that spans research, clinical practice and commercial silos.

With these ten characteristics in mind, let's explore just a few of the many opportunities that advanced analytics and a stronger data science can offer.

TARGET IMPROVEMENT AREAS
Clinical Research Optimization

Advanced analytics enable life sciences organizations to execute more efficient and less expensive clinical trials than ever before. Innovative trial designs that reduce the number of trials, optimized strategies to allocate resources, and more accurate and reliable patient recruitment are among the many ways that applying advanced analytics to clinical trials can fundamentally improve their execution.

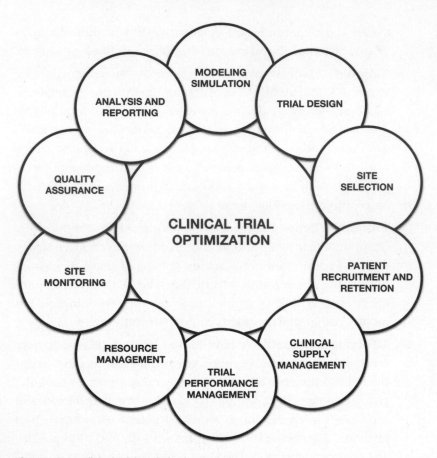

Figure 13.3 Clinical Trial Optimization Domains.

As illustrated in Figure 13.3, clinical research optimization as a domain covers a very large collection of capabilities and process improvement areas representing the entire lifecycle of clinical research: study design, location, patient recruitment, supply chain management, resourcing, and many other issues. Today, much of this work is: a) manual, b) retrospective, and c) disconnected from the dependencies that ultimately determine what happens. As an industry, we have decades of experience covering tens of thousands of clinical trials to draw from—why would we ever "guess" where the patients are, what investigators produce the most reliable research performance, which data suffers from quality problems, what research designs are most efficient, and how to forecast clinical trial materials and drug supplies?

In recent years, interest in "adaptive clinical trials" has grown as a potential way to expedite clinical research. Much of the industry has used the concepts in adaptive clinical trials for years, but sustainable performance improvements have been hampered by:

- Confusion over readiness by regulators
- Lack of education on how best to apply the techniques
- Shortage of effective software tools to facilitate adaptive methodologies

But many of these issues have solutions today: regulators have published guidance, educational opportunities abound, and software tools exist. So the timing is excellent for developing stronger competencies in clinical trials optimization.

From an analytics perspective, opportunities in adaptive clinical trial methodologies fall into two general categories (see Figure 13.4):

1. **Research Design Improvements**—using statistical approaches such as study simulation to optimize the research design and study execution parameters. Poorly designed trials are a waste of money and time, and border on unethical. Companies have the data to inform designs with a high likelihood of success; by leveraging these assets with advanced analytics, companies

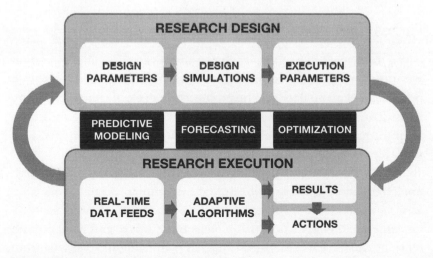

Figure 13.4 Adaptive Trial Improvement Areas.

can reduce their costs, decrease their time to market, and meet the ethical demands of clinical research.

2. **Research Execution Improvements**—using analytics against real-time clinical and administrative data feeds to ensure that the study runs efficiently and effectively. Historically, the industry has relied on dedicated, manual software systems for project management, trial management, materials management, and performance management. In a world of real-time data, there is absolutely no need to track status and performance information manually—analytics (even basic descriptive statistics) can not only reduce the burdens associated with clinical trials execution, but they do it in a way that: a) is more accurate, and b) builds a longer-term data asset that can be used for subsequent trial improvements.

Like so many intelligent applications of advanced analytics, these improvements are recursive, providing increasingly more powerful returns on investment over time. Design optimizations are in effect "tested" in the real world of study execution. The results from those process "experiments" are then used in subsequent research design optimizations. Tomorrow's "learning health system" can start today with a "learning health research system."

Process Automation

Given the remarkable sophistication of devices such as cell phones that we use every day, it is shocking how much of the clinical research process is still manual today. The proliferation of electronic data capture tools (EDCs) for collecting patient data has helped ease the transition from forms to transactional databases, but those improvements have not scaled to other process areas.

Our industry needs to move towards a "closed-loop" research implementation process, as illustrated in Figure 13.5. Data collection forms should derive from standards and practices related to protocol implementations—practices that have been shown over time to be both efficient and effective. Statistical analysis plans should be derived from those same protocols using similar performance-based criteria. As the

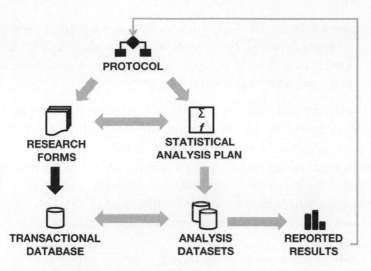

Figure 13.5 Research Process Automation Opportunity.

research process unfolds, reported results are linked directly back to their respective areas of the protocol. Not only does this serve the need of showing traceability and deriving performance improvements over time, it also treats the problem of "extraneous data" that we will discuss in a moment.

Structured Research Models and Intelligent Standards

One of the biggest challenges in reusability relates to structured representations of research models and context. Today, research study designs are described in unstructured word processing documents. Though useful for human collaboration and review, unstructured research documents cannot easily be linked to their corresponding data. This produces several problems:

1. Since information on the research design is not in a computable form (meaning that computers cannot consistently interpret the details of the designs), it becomes impossible to automate the activities that are articulated in the protocol.

2. The protocol is where clinical context is defined. As such, it should be used to assign "planned context" (i.e., what a measurement was

intended to cover) of any data collected during the trial.[1] Without a structured electronic representation of clinical context, it becomes extremely difficult to reuse clinical data for meta-analysis or more predictive analytical applications.

Within the past 10 years, considerable progress has been made in the development of technical standards designed to facilitate the exchange of clinical data. Unfortunately, most of the effort has been spent in trying to figure out how to exchange data rather than actually use it once it is received. Nevertheless, efforts such as the Clinical Data Interchange Standards Consortium (CDISC) and Health Level 7 (HL7) have provided some foundational elements critical to facilitating clinical integration.

Going forward, organizations need to invest in this level of standards work in ways that have not been pursued to date. Industry architectures are needed to connect cross-enterprise processes and workflows. Standards need to be self-describing, where machines can communicate what standards they use and how they can be deployed without extensive human intervention. And perhaps most importantly, consistent mechanisms for representing clinical context must be deployed. Technologies already available—XML, semantic Web, Web services, and others—have the technical capabilities needed to implement these improvements today, just as they have been implemented in other industries (e.g., EDI and automotive supply chains). Technical architects and information scientists know how to do this work; industry leaders just need to refuse to accept today's *status quo*.

Clinical Portfolio Management

Status quo also plagues the process by which research institutions manage their portfolios of R&D investments. In describing how portfolio management techniques can be applied to clinical research, I was once told by an industry executive, "Yes, I know you are right, it would help. But our firm would never do that. We have a whole management team who have built their careers on gut-based decisions." I wanted to say, "Is that the same management team that cannot seem to fix your product pipeline problem? Anyone think these two issues might be connected?"

The pharmaceutical industry is not the only industry that carries investment portfolios. It is not the only industry that tries to manage risk and uncertainty in those portfolios. But it is one of the few industries that have not acknowledged that predictive analytics can help.

In the pharmaceutical implementation of portfolio management, organizations can rationalize a top-down view of optimization opportunities with a bottom-up view of historical and current information. In doing so, they can improve both strategic and tactical decision making. Data models bridging R&D and commercial information sources can provide better visibility into the risk-versus-rewards tradeoffs. And data from individual research projects—the same data used in our examples above—provide the foundation for understanding how performance and risks are unfolding in real time.

Truly Open Innovation

Much of what the pharmaceutical industry has evangelized as "open innovation" has really been a stronger partnering business model. Due to costs, commercial considerations, and risks, it has been difficult to establish fundamentally new models of drug discovery and development. But ample opportunities exist for those willing to try something new.

In other market segments, we have seen the emergence of entirely new models of product research, customer engagement, and funding (see Figure 13.6).

The "open innovation challenges" sponsored by a few of the top pharmaceutical companies have been great examples of the

Figure 13.6 New Models for Innovation.

opportunities in unlocking the corporate doors to new ideas and customer feedback. Are there others?

- Could we see models where patients band together to support and participate in research into niche therapies that would otherwise be unprofitable?

- With a more cost-effective research process, can crowd-sourced funding models offset or even cover the development costs of novel therapies?

- Can more creative alliances between drug developers, academic medical institutions, community providers, payers, and regulators accelerate therapy development by removing barriers to accessing patients, data, and funding?

- Can the "signal detection" approach used in combinatorial chemistry and high-throughput screening be applied to broad patient medical records set to search for latent signals in treatment options?

- Can national health, drug, and safety surveillance efforts create information assets that offer insights into possible mechanisms of action for diseases, biological agents, and/or drugs? What new opportunities in comparative effectiveness research does this unlock?

THE DATA CONUNDRUM

The approach we have advocated in this book has included a strong focus on data—more, broader, higher quality, and used more creatively. But in the case of drug development, this approach faces a challenge.

Clinical trials already collect very large quantities of data, and much of the data is not really needed. It is estimated that clinical trials spend $4–6 billion annually collecting extraneous data (i.e., data related to procedures for supplementary secondary, tertiary, and exploratory endpoints). This extraneous data accounts for around 18% of clinical trial budgets, which means on average each study spends over $1 million on this data.[2]

Why do researchers do this? The two reasons most commonly cited are "well, we don't know if it will show something important" and "regulators might ask about it." If these reasons evoke a sense of *déjà vu*, you may be recalling the provider-market concept of "defensive medicine" where medical practitioners order cost-escalating patient tests "just to make sure." Rest assured that "defensive research" is alive and well.

Having said that, there is a financial argument to be made for extraneous data: it is cheaper to do it now than later. Delaying market launch for a new product could cost the company $1 million a day in revenue. In other words, many consider extraneous data collection to be insurance—better to pay a little now than face paying much more later.

Nevertheless, extraneous or "noncore" data collection leads to several problems. Obviously, one problem is increased R&D costs, which inevitably translates into higher drug costs for patients and payers. Another is research timelines. As it takes time to collect, clean, and analyze all of this extra data, products take longer to get to market, reducing the company's revenue, delaying patient interventions, and prolonging human suffering. And a third challenge is opportunity cost—people and money allocated to collecting unimportant data are unable to contribute to pursuing more meaningful innovations.

Most pharmaceutical companies have become more aware of the issues with extraneous data collection, and have introduced at least awareness campaigns and new best practice policies within their clinical development divisions to combat the problem. But "banning" extraneous data collection is not the answer. More constructive options for dealing with extraneous data collection include:

- **Reduce Unmanaged Decisions.** The real issue is not whether organizations collect too much extraneous information. The real issue is that the decisions on noncore data expenditures are not well managed. Better discrimination of when, what, how much, and why to go beyond core data and endpoints is needed. Analytical techniques such as modeling, forecasting, and simulation can assist in assessing the time and cost implications of collecting additional data.

- **Increase Collaborative Decision Making.** Since a lot of extraneous data collection is related to ambiguity in regulatory expectations, one approach to limiting this issue is closer collaboration between regulators and researchers. It is probably unrealistic to think that regulators or researchers can predict with complete certainty what data will ultimately be needed to support market approval. But developing mutually-agreed-to contingency plans to proactively address emerging issues should provide both organizations with greater confidence that all of the concerns can and will be addressed. Analytics can be used to determine and justify the "triggers" for making subsequent investments in data collection.

- **Pursue Parallel Investigations.** If a drug's primary safety and efficacy endpoints (including comparative effectiveness) are insufficient to justify market approval and formulary inclusion, no amount of secondary, tertiary, and exploratory data will justify continuing with the current development plan. Removing those noncore data activities and endpoints from the "critical path" of a drug's development life cycle makes a lot of sense. We gain financial benefits from postponing those expenses, and the investigation of the noncore endpoints may actually be accelerated through parallel studies. In addition, subsequent core data may address the questions and considerations being explored in the noncore data.

- **Determine Analytically What is Important.** Whether through meta-analyses, simulations, surrogate endpoints, or observational studies, there are many analytical options to help us in determining whether a data element or endpoint is likely to be important. We may not need to actually run an empirical study, especially if both researchers and regulators agree that the analytical evidence does not suggest subsequent dedicated data collection will produce more meaningful insights.

- **Implement Activity-Based Costing (again).** Industry estimates of extraneous data collection impacts are derived from reasonably high-level estimates of expenditures. Historically, it has been difficult to assess the relative impact of extraneous data collection alongside other major sources of clinical research delays and costs. For example, we know that over half of study protocols are amended at least once after the study starts, and that each change typically takes more than 60 days to resolve.[3] So whereas extraneous data collection is a problem, it may not be the most urgent. The same analytical approaches discussed earlier in this book relating to cost and activity analysis—methodologies and tools such as activity-based costing, for example—can give us greater visibility into how we should prioritize research process reengineering efforts to optimize time and outcomes.

In the end, we also have to acknowledge that some waste is always expected in R&D. There will always be suboptimal data collection; if we knew all the answers, it would not be called "research."

To that end, we also have to acknowledge that the health analytics approach being promoted in this book will definitely increase the collection of data that is ultimately found not useful in predicting clinical efficacy and safety. But that is the point! Explicitly ruling "in" or "out" the relevance of a data dimension should be exactly what R&D is about. It is not the predictive value of data that makes it extraneous; it is whether the data is collected for a truly defensible reason. If the answer is "no, this factor is not important," and that answer helps us understand real dimensions of the drug—who should use it, what outcome it will produce, how we can optimize the outcome, how it performs against comparative therapies, etc.—then the goals of R&D towards personalized medicine are served.

THE BIG FOUR

The new data-oriented science we are describing here is rich with opportunities. But we cannot just ignore the limitations and risks inherent in these approaches as well.

The top three risks most commonly associated with these types of data-oriented investigations are as follows:

1. **Sampling Bias.** There is always a risk—particularly in conditions uncontrolled by scientific methods—that the individuals being analyzed are not representative of the broader population of patients. They may not be diverse enough, for example, so we may not observe critical issues related to outcomes and risks.

2. **Completeness.** The process of developing a controlled experiment includes careful consideration of what really needs to be measured in order to feel confident that our experimental findings will be conclusive. In scenarios where we are analyzing data already collected, and using that data for purposes not originally intended, there is a risk that we have not measured and/or analyzed the most important things.

3. **Repeatability.** The controls we use in scientific experiments allow those experiments to be subsequently reproduced by other scientists, and this reproducibility is a critical requirement of good science. Without those controls, it may be difficult if not impossible to exactly reproduce the effects observed in our data. Though statisticians have mathematical methods for exploring repeatability within and across data sets, there is no substitute for experimental methods.

For these three reasons, we will not escape our ultimate reliance on the scientific method any time soon. Our data-oriented investigations can and should serve to stage subsequent controlled experiments— exploring the repeatability, ensuring broader sampling accuracy, and collecting a broad enough set of data to establish confidence in our findings. Note, though, that these same risks are risks within controlled experimental conditions as well; we are not describing new risks to our investigations, we are describing elevated risks.

But there is one new risk that comes with this data science:

4. **Constraints.** By defining the precise methods and data collection practices used, controlled experiments provide us the limitations around our data. In interpreting our analyses and results, we know a lot about the data: where it came from, how recently it was checked for accuracy, what assumptions were made during data generation, confidence intervals of the machines

used, assumptions on "normal" versus "abnormal" readings, and the context of the data observations themselves. We usually know none of these things when dealing with data coming from outside our controlled experiments. As mentioned briefly earlier in the book, our lack of visibility to data pedigree and clinical context limits the utility of both the data and the analyses.

As we look to scale up our data science investigations over the coming decades, these risk-related issues likely indicate the need for us to develop an "analytical method"—a statistical corollary to the "scientific method" that allows us to articulate what is known and unknown about our data. Such a framework would help us mitigate the four risks described here—sampling bias, completeness, repeatability, and constraints—by offering a standardized framework for capturing and communicating "data about our data." If the era of big data represents an era of lost context and pedigree, any instrument to help control the tradeoffs we make when relying on explorations other than through the scientific method would be valuable.

ONE THAT DOES WHAT IT SHOULD

By now, it is probably clear that our scope of research needs to grow In this book, we have shown how it is not possible, practical, or advisable to continue to separate provider, payer, and life sciences market concerns into silos—zero-sum economics do not work. We've discussed how the efficacy and safety of medical treatments is about a lot more than the drug compound or treatment protocol; if we want good health outcomes for each patient, we must more comprehensively assess all of the factors related to health outcomes for that individual patient. We've talked about the need for greater performance management and cost controls in order to drive a more profitable health economy.

Generally speaking, R&D does not cover a lot of these topics today. Our R&D efforts have focused on the sciences of biology and chemistry. We are now asking the science to grow and incorporate many other disciplines: management sciences, psychology, and cost accounting to name a few. The road ahead does not look like the road behind.

But this is what personalized medicine should become. Personal should not mean generic. It should not mean smaller versions of population health. It should mean *personalized*—best suited to the individual patient receiving the care. That's what patients and doctors want. It is what prevents unnecessary medical complications and expenses. It is what drives deeper insights into how we might cure and not just treat disease. It produces more productive workforces, and it reduces human suffering.

In 1984, the American pop/rock band Huey Lewis and the News had a top ten hit song called "I Want a New Drug." In it, the singer enumerates the attributes of his ideal treatment, including that it won't make him sick, feel three feet thick, hurt his head, make his mouth too dry, make his eyes too red, doesn't cost too much, won't go away, won't keep him up all night or make him sleep all day . . . "one that does what it should." When our medical research can deliver treatments that satisfy Mr. Lewis' criteria, we will know that we have reached personalized medicine.

Carl Sagan was in many ways a model for where our new medical R&D needs to go. Though most famous for his work on the educational TV series "Cosmos," Sagan was not constrained by conventional definitions of a scientist. His contributions spanned multiple fields including astronomy, astrophysics, exobiology, cosmology, and genetics. Contributing to more than 600 publications during his lifetime, he was a multidisciplinary freethinker who let data and scientific inquiry guide his thinking in areas scientifically unconventional such as the search for extraterrestrial intelligence. His passion for science and the search for truth was unparalleled.

In his later years, Sagan contracted a disease called myelodysplasia, a blood disorder related to bone marrow stem cells. Science has not yet uncovered the causes or a cure for the disease. But like so many other diseases, we know a few fragments of interesting information; for example, this one manifests more frequently in males and adults over 60. And we know that the currently available treatments (i.e., bone marrow transplants, blood transfusions) impact patients differently, though we cannot easily predict how. Sagan had three bone marrow transplants, but the corresponding compromises to his immune system led to his eventual death from pneumonia less than a year after publishing *The Demon-Haunted World*. At 62, he was relatively young, though thanks to science, quite old compared to his Alexandrian forefathers.

NOTES

1. Note: Representing "planned" versus "actual" is a long-standing clinical data management debate, and one that we will avoid duplicating here. Suffice it to say that clinical data needs to represent both—what was the original plan for collecting a data point, and what was the actual context in which was collected.
2. "November/December CSDD Impact Report," Tufts Center for the Study of Drug Development, November 2012. http://csdd.tufts.edu
3. "September/October Tufts CSDD Impact Report," Tufts Center for the Study of Drug Development, September 2011. http://csdd.tufts.edu

CHAPTER **14**
Conclusions

Well, you made it through a book on analytics, and hopefully it was even enjoyable at times. I kept my promise of not drilling into detailed-level math and statistics with the slight exception of our discussion of value (and be honest, you would have been disappointed if a book on analytics didn't have at least one Greek letter in it somewhere, especially since the opening story is about Alexandria).

This book set out to look at different ways health and life sciences could become smarter through the use of information and analytics. In truth, we've only scratched the surface. Perhaps as you read through the ideas presented here, you had a momentary thought of "Wait, couldn't we also do _____?" or "Why wouldn't _____fit here?" There really is so much opportunity; no one book could capture it all.

Some aspects of the book may seem critical of our industry's existing use of data, technology, and analytics, but that really was not the intention. We simply want to "upgrade" the quality of the questions we are asking across health and life sciences. We don't need to constrain ourselves to retrospective analyses—we could build prospective analytical models. We don't have to manage thousands of quality measures—we would use analytics to figure out what is actually important. We don't have to struggle getting insights out of the limited sets of data behind our firewalls—we could collaboratively develop insights. We don't have to wait for decades-long research to pursue personalized medicine and identify best practices—we can use analytics to provide more evidence-based care today. The quality of the answers we get are completely dependent on the quality of the questions we ask, and there are a lot of questions that we could be asking—and should be asking— that will more effectively lead us to a value-driven health and life sciences ecosystem.

Linking clinical, financial, administrative, and personal perspectives together in more comprehensive models of health performance gives us something fundamentally new: the foundation by which we can pursue value-based innovation, not simply operational tweaks to existing business models and processes (i.e., ones that we already know are not well suited to achieve our long-term goals). Figure 14.1 illustrates this new foundation for analytics-driven innovation.

It remains to be seen how "disruptive" this innovation will be, or whether it will be driven by large institutions or smaller, more agile organizations. The pharmaceutical mergers of the 1990s taught us that bigger is not necessarily better for pursuing innovation and driving efficiency. And that pattern may be repeating itself in the ongoing consolidation within and across the provider and payer markets. We cannot simply buy or contract new models of health value delivery— they have to be built.

So how do we get started?

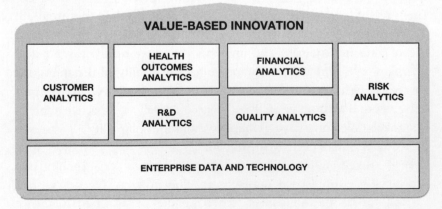

Figure 14.1 Analytics Supporting Value-Based Innovation.

TAKING ON RESEARCH

The first step in pursuing this innovation is acknowledging that it looks fundamentally different than what many in our industry do today. It is largely a journey into the unknown.

Journeys into the unknown can be fun and exciting. But they are not for everyone; they can be risky and scary to many. So we will need to be selective in picking our team of explorers, and we will need to treat them a little differently than other areas of the business.

What do these explorers look like? Obviously, the brave, curious, and entrepreneurial will find pleasure in this work. A tolerance for ambiguity is absolutely critical. Team size is really a matter of organizational priority and preference (five is a good number), but regardless of size, our explorers will need some specific skills in order to complete their mission:

- **Subject matter expertise** in the business and/or clinical topic (e.g., a disease management expert). This person will often function as a surrogate for the eventual business customer, as they have a very clear understanding of what will be useful. Ideally, this person can lead the team.

- **Advanced analytical expertise**, such as technical skills in building predictive models within statistical software. On a per-project basis, this expertise will often be in two forms: generalists who can provide the bulk of analytical needs, and specialists in particular analytical methods and techniques (e.g., optimization) that offer unique value to the question being explored.

- **Data expertise**, especially some knowledge of the source data systems and data structures available. Ideally, this person will have a background in data integration, data quality, and database administration.

- **Project management** to keep everything moving. Ideally, the project manager would have experience in agile software development practices (discussed later in this section).

In some analytical scenarios, technical expertise in high-performance computing may also be useful, especially when the problem space involves very large data sets or highly complex mathematical algorithms. But most problems can be explored without focusing too heavily on how quickly and reliably computing resources are processing the work.

With these profiles and skills as backdrop, how does this exploratory work get delivered? Stated simply, every health and life sciences organization of significant size needs an informatics research group focused on innovation. Many will argue this point: organizational size, budget, skill sets, and many other reasons will be offered as to why informatics research and development (R&D) is not in their business model. But the alternative—business as usual—is much more risky than investing in informatics because we know with a high degree of certainty that business as usual is not financially viable. Portions of the research work can absolutely be outsourced, so this does not imply large-scale growth in human resource or capital costs. But it does require some investment, including someone to own it within the organization (it is usually not advisable to completely outsource your own business strategy).

However it is resourced, this innovation research function should be designed with a couple of things in mind. First, one of the reasons for forming a discrete research group and research process is risk management. Research contains risk, and some of the research efforts will fail (if they don't, we are likely not being as innovative as we could). We do not want those risks and failures compromising the operational business; otherwise, we run the risk of exacerbating the cost, quality, and outcome issues we are trying to improve. So we need a way of partitioning the risk, and creating a dedicated function helps to do that.

Second, it is important that this innovation function be granted some degree of freedom in terms of business process and culture. Leaders should not seek to build an innovation function that looks, acts, and feels like the existing business. At the same time, if the function deviates too far from "the mothership," it will be difficult to align and integrate the new capabilities into the operational environment. So it is a difficult balancing act.

Third, any time a dedicated research, innovation, or emerging business unit is formed, there is a risk that the function and the people are perceived as an "ivory tower"—a group of people off doing things without proper perspective and buy-in from the real world. Such a perception makes it extremely difficult for the team to be effective, so ensuring proper engagement across the organization is crucial. Techniques for doing this include transparent and frequent communication; operational feedback and input on projects; soliciting operational staff for improvement ideas and priorities; collaborative goal setting with management; and temporarily assigning operational staff to innovation project teams.

And finally, it is very important that the new research process include a clear definition of delivery expectations. In any R&D effort, you can simultaneously lock down only two factors among the big three—time, people, and scope. For most health organizations, the people will be fixed; there will only be a certain number of people allocated to the research function, so they define capacity). That means that an organization can elect to fix scope (meaning that the organization is willing to invest however much time is needed in order to deliver a certain capability), or they can elect to fix time (meaning that the team will deliver whatever capabilities can be delivered in the timeframe allotted).

In most health and life sciences settings, it is probably preferable to lock down the time; tasking teams to get done whatever can be achieved in a particular timeframe. Fixed-time delivery processes have been very successful in "agile" software development, a development process that provides for iterative delivery of incremental software capabilities. Though this book does not deal with any specific operational methodologies, it is safe to assume that the use of formalized agile methods can greatly contribute to project success, as they are designed to manage the realities of unknowns within a project. They also explicitly plan for the fact that the development of capabilities is iterative, something we expect to be true of all advanced analytical models. Time-based delivery also helps control any team tendencies towards perfectionism, opting instead for the idea that delivering something on time is preferable to pursuing ideal solutions. By their very nature, analytical research projects can go on forever—there are always more questions to ask and research to undertake. So fixed delivery dates keep people focused on business value.

FIVE PHASES OF VALUE-BASED ANALYTICAL INNOVATION

Figure 14.2 illustrates a five-phase process through which analytical innovation projects can be managed.

Each of the phases involves successively more organizational commitment to the analytical capability being pursued. But those commitments are matched at each phase transition by evidence justifying continued investment (or a decision to halt).

Phase 1: Research. During this phase, a small team of experts is brought together for purposes of exploring the topic. Ideally, this team will be multidisciplinary, as many of the questions under research will cover multiple domains of knowledge. The goal of this phase is to collect what is known, clarify what is unknown, and build a plan for proving both the feasibility and value of the new analytical capability. The time frame for this work can vary based on the complexity of the question being asked, but three months is a reasonable time frame— beyond that, and you probably need to deconstruct the question into smaller, more manageable chunks of work. Note that it is possible to research a topic and decide not to pursue it further—that is not a failure, it is a legitimate finding.

Phase 2: Prove. The goal of this phase is simple: generate evidence that a new analytical model works and is superior to existing approaches to answering the question. We don't need the model or answer to be perfect, but we want to make sure further investment in the analytical approach is warranted. Assuming the organization is using a fixed time frame for delivery, this phase will likely be the first place that the time frame will be challenged, as teams will want to prove more aspects than time will allow. That is often a good thing—it means the team understands the problem space. The Prove phase should be all about risk management; in particular, removing risk of the largest unknowns. Whatever aspects of the project are most ambiguous should be what gets clarified here, and there should be no question as to the value of the solution by the time the proof

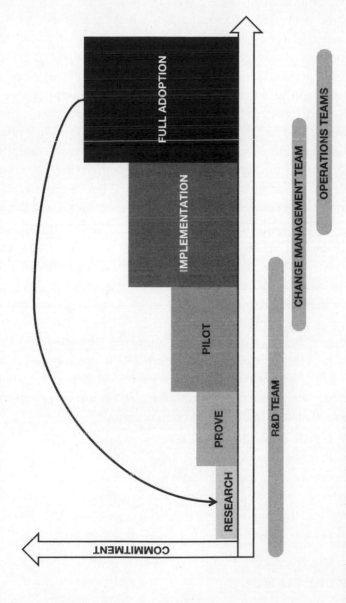

Figure 14.2 Five Phases of Analytical Innovation.

231

exercise is completed. Proof phases of two–three months fit well, and reflect common practices in software development as well.

Phase 3: Pilot. Assuming we are successful in the proof, the next phase is focused on learning how those capabilities and their value might be deployed. The focus here begins to cross over into operational concerns: how would this be deployed?; what improvements and capabilities are needed?; and what are the barriers? This is the first phase where ongoing business operations are impacted by the project, and the risk exposure is "ring-fenced" to a small number of people involved in the Pilot phase. Assuming the pilot is successful, a crucial deliverable from this phase is the implementation plan. The length of Pilot projects can vary dramatically based on solution area, but in general, pilots lasting longer than six months can become confusing and diluted.

Phase 4: Implementation. During the Implementation phase, we deploy the new capabilities into the operational areas of the business. There are lots of data and technology implications to implementing a new solution, but the challenges in this phase are more about change management. Individuals and groups across the organization need help in transitioning to the insights being offered through analytics. Education and clear management expectations are crucial to the success of this phase. Implementation timeframes should follow the implementation plan; variance from the plan represents operational risks that should obviously be managed.

Phase 5: Full Adoption. Once the new capability is deployed, the work is not done. Analytical models can be improved. New data sources become available. Data quality issues surface that need to be resolved. And new issues and insights are uncovered that become the subject of new research projects. This phase is where the "learning health system" becomes realized.

PHASE 0: THE PLAN

Of course, in order to execute our five-phase approach, you need one more thing: agreement on what to pursue. And the list of options is endless.

Early in the book, we presented the idea of an analytical capability map—a collection of the critical analytical competencies for the organization, as well as an assessment of the current operating levels and management priorities. This map serves as the foundation for "picking your targets"—identifying those innovation areas that should get priority. We also presented the idea of strategy maps and scorecards—established frameworks for developing, executing, and monitoring performance and performance improvements. During the Planning phase, these two maps get connected, as illustrated in Figure 14.3.

The strategy map and scorecard lay out the priorities for the organization. Analytical competencies should support those objectives. Within the framework of the balanced scorecard, for example, analytical projects focused on developing new capabilities exist as part of the Projects portion of the scorecard framework. The development and implementation of these new capabilities should serve to advance the business objective(s) for which the project is associated.

In this way, health analytics become tied to business performance. At the core of this concept is the idea that the business strategy should be at the center of organizational activities and investments. In the information-driven world that health analytics offers, the business strategy is supported by an information strategy that articulates the insights necessary to operate the business in a more evidence-oriented way. This information strategy, in turn, requires an analytical strategy to deliver those insights. And all of the above—the business strategy, the information strategy, and the analytics strategy—unify clinical, financial, administrative, and customer dimensions of analytics and insights (see Figure 14.4).

MANAGING CAPABILITY MATURITY

Of course, the scope of what we have just described is huge. How should an industry leader pursue such a comprehensive set of capability developments, especially given the cost constraints driving the industry today?

Organizations can only handle so much change. And with limited capacity in resources, there is a finite (and usually quite small) capacity available for innovation. Though the strategy and planning work

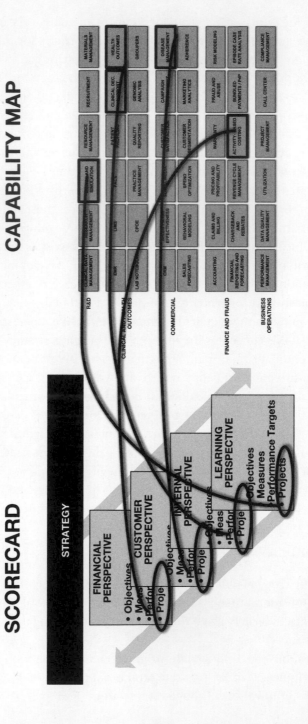

Figure 14.3 Linking a Balanced Scorecard to a Corresponding Capability Map.

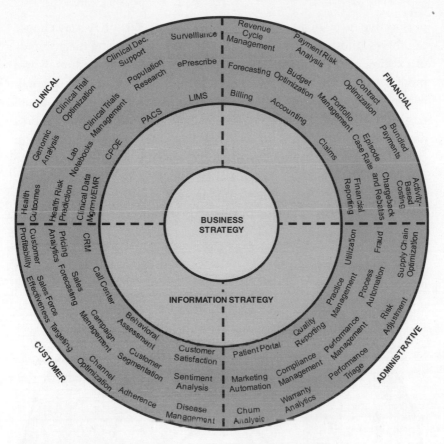

Figure 14.4 Linking Business, Information, and Analytical Strategies.

usually needs to be taken on as a comprehensive exercise, the actual analytical projects should be pursued at a more moderate pace.

In the early days of analytical growth, an organization doesn't necessarily see or understand the limitations of its own data until they try to pursue analytics. Time and capacity will be needed to "learn what we don't know," and remediate the internal issues uncovered. By taking the time to learn these issues up front, subsequent analytical projects can benefit from the experience.

Another reason to start small and grow is that a given analytical capability can grow over time in both depth (i.e., power, accuracy, related functionality) as well as breadth (i.e., linking to other question topics). For example, if an organization decides to pursue a financial perspective through an activity-based costing project, they may choose to progress those capabilities deeper over time, improving the accuracy of existing costing models, or exploring more sophisticated analytical models that might offer more powerful insights into cost accrual. Alternatively, the same assets created as part of the activity-based costing effort could subsequently be linked to clinical and claims data to begin exploring how costs and outcomes are related from the clinical perspective. By studying a single problem space from multiple angles (see Figure 14.5), organizations can gain immediate leverage from prior investments while simultaneously creating additional capabilities that will be leveraged in subsequent projects.

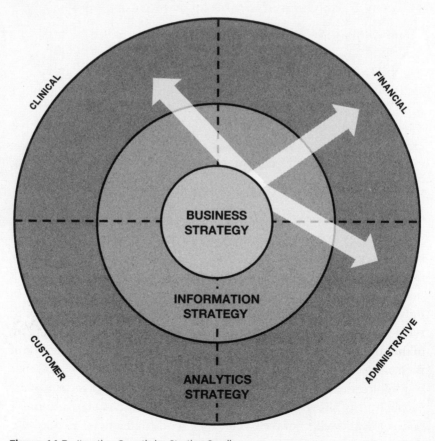

Figure 14.5 Iterative Growth by Starting Small.

In the end, though, the answer to what is the right way is, "It depends." There is no right or wrong answer in general—only what is appropriate and effective for a particular organization. As is true with so many change and growth initiatives, the management challenges are likely more cultural and logistical than technical:

- Building new governance models to drive consensus on strategy, priorities, and projects
- Creating a culture open to new insights coming from "statistics" as opposed to traditional research
- Developing tolerance and rewards even for failures
- Making investment tradeoff decisions
- Overcoming organizational skill and resourcing gaps

It won't be easy. But it will be rewarding.

WISDOM AND HEALTH

Returning one last time to Alexandria: Herophilos' groundbreaking work in anatomy and the scientific method set a new course for medicine. As a medical innovator, he cofounded the great medical school at Alexandria with a colleague named Erasistratus, and these two men collaborated on many topics in anatomy. Erasistratus was the first to determine that the heart actually served as a pump. He differentiated between sensory and motor neurons, and discovered that they were connected to the brain. He was one of the first scientists to ever study the cerebrum and cerebellum.

Most detailed information and works of Herophilos and Erasistratus have been lost to time, so we cannot say for certain what their working relationship was like. But it seems obvious, both from their cofounding of the Alexandrian medical school as well as the exponential growth of their contributions, that theirs was a fruitful collaboration. Though Herophilos and Erasistratus became two of the earliest anatomists, they each brought slightly different perspectives to the investigations. If collaboration was not at the heart of these rapid advances in medicine, it undoubtedly was a catalyst.

Herophilos is credited with stating:

> When health is absent,
> wisdom cannot reveal itself,
> art cannot manifest,
> strength cannot fight,
> wealth becomes useless,
> and intelligence cannot be applied.

Today, we think the opposite may also be true: when wisdom is absent, health cannot reveal itself. We cannot bring about a stronger position of human health without greater understanding, and that greater understanding comes in the face of growing volumes of data that exceed our ability to independently draw conclusions. It may be that one day we will be able to reduce the complexity of medicine into a few easily understood laws of medicine—our equivalent to physics' "theory of everything." But physics has yet to develop and prove a theory of everything; the unification of quantum mechanics and general relativity eludes our present understanding of the universe.

The comparison of the quantum-relativity paradox is strikingly similar to what we face in health care. General relativity explains the behavior of large objects, much in the same way that population-oriented health research explains medicine across large groups. Quantum physics, however, explains things happening at a very small scale, just as personalized medicine explains health outcomes at the level of the individual. Just as general relativity and quantum mechanics are not mutually exclusive—they both have strong evidence in their support—so we see that population-level health dynamics and more individualized health can coexist. The forces at play differ, and they both warrant exploration. And today, theories of quantum physics are now developed with one eye towards the implications in general relativity, and vice versa.

If our hypotheses about health analytics are correct—if complexity does now exceed cognition, if the exponential growth in data unlocks new opportunities for analytically-derived insights, and if patient centricity is all about using this information collaboratively to make more personalized decisions—our industry stands at the edge of a new wave of health improvements. The road ahead truly does not look like the road behind. And through our care innovations and practices, we can surpass papyrus-like technologies and volume-based business models. We can deliver what patients deserve. We can find our way out of the dark.

About the Author

Jason Burke is the founder of Burke Advisory Group, an executive consulting firm focused on helping health leaders pursue transformational programs using data, technology, and analytics. He holds a visiting faculty appointment with the University Of North Carolina Chapel Hill School Of Medicine, where he focuses on the development of new health informatics capabilities for health practitioners, researchers, and patients. Burke's passions include strategy development, emerging business design, and information and technology innovation.

Previously, Burke was the Managing Director and Chief Strategist for the SAS Center for Health Analytics & Insights (CHAI), coordinating the development and execution of SAS's industry strategy and emerging solutions portfolio across health care provider, health plan, pharmaceutical, biotechnology, and regulatory organizations around the world. He led the software firm's health and life sciences research and development organization, and founded the company's health and life sciences Global Practice. Prior to joining SAS, Burke developed emerging business areas for GlaxoSmithKline (GSK), Quintiles Transnational, and Microsoft. He has served as a technology leader in several industry think tank and strategic development initiatives focusing on the future of health care and pharmaceutical research. Burke is active in online social media, including a blog (http://JasonBurke.us), LinkedIn, Facebook, and Twitter.

Index

V